A Mindful Way
Eight Weeks to Happiness

A Mindful Way

EIGHT WEEKS TO HAPPINESS

Jeanie Seward-Magee

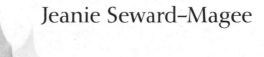

PARALLAX PRESS
BERKELEY, CA

Parallax Press
P.O. Box 7355
Berkeley, California 94707
www.parallax.org

Parallax Press is the publishing division of Unified Buddhist Church, Inc.

Edited by Rachel Neumann.
Cover design by Charles Woods.
Text design by Gopa & Ted 2, Inc.

Library of Congress Cataloging-in-Publication Data

Seward-Magee, Jeanie.
   A mindful way : eight weeks to happiness / Jeanie Seward-Magee.
     p. cm.
   ISBN 1-888375-58-2 (pbk.)
   1. Meditation. 2. Happiness—Religious aspects. 3. Self-help techniques.
4. Five Precepts (Buddhism)   I. Title.
   BL627.S49 2006
   204'.4—dc22

                                                          2006019249

1 2 3 4 5 / 10 09 08 07 06

www.amindfulway.com

This book is dedicated to
John, David, Mark, Timothy,
Larissa, Angela, and Amanda.

Table of Contents

Foreword

A Mindful Way is a simple and effective introduction to the moral and spiritual guide called The Five Mindfulness Trainings. It offers creative ideas for daily practical exercises and activities that can help bring about inner peace, unselfishness, understanding, tolerance, and compassion.

We can often become victims of our own minds—paralyzed by regret about the past and fear of the future. To live in grace, truly at peace with ourselves, requires deep insight and changing our behavior to reflect that insight.

Through the practices of daily meditation, journaling, and expressing gratitude, *A Mindful Way* enables readers to seek and find their own insights, deepening their understanding of themselves and others.

The present moment is the most precious gift we have. *A Mindful Way* is a simple guide to help each of us enjoy and appreciate every moment we are given.

–Thich Nhat Hanh

TONIGHT

THE MOON REFLECTS

ON TOMORROW'S MORNING GLORY

W · E · E · K   O · N · E

Beginning Your Mindful Journey

Each of us seeks peace, joy, and freedom in the present moment. No matter what our childhood was like or where we grew up, we all experienced, for at least a little while, the wonder of living in the moment when we were children. However, as adults, our lives are often now spent regretting our past or worrying about our future. Is this the way you wish to live your life? We have a choice whether to live at Ground Zero, constantly in the center of a crisis, or to be grounded in mindfulness. Whatever the circumstances of our life, this choice is completely up to us.

With *A Mindful Way*—and eight weeks of practice—you can receive the gifts of greater acceptance, understanding, peace, and freedom. I hope they will become some of the most treasured gifts you have ever given yourself.

Leading a more peaceful and conscious life is not simply a matter of reading this book, doing the exercises, and hoping that life will become better. Leading a mindful life is about daily practice. When we want to do anything well in life, we have to practice each and every day. The world's greatest musicians and athletes have practiced daily to become accomplished in their chosen professions. So if you choose to become a more mindful and aware human being, one of the first things you must accept is that it will

3

take moment-by-moment practice for the rest of your life. This is not an easy task, but it is a joyful one.

A Mindful Way can be the first step on a path that will lead to a new way of living for you. It may help you achieve what in Zen Buddhism is called Beginner's Mind, the ability to open up your eyes, ears, speech, and heart to a new way of approaching your life.

What Is Mindfulness?

Mindfulness is another word for having a clear mind, a mind that is fully conscious in each present moment. It teaches us to look deeply at ourselves and at the world. Mindfulness can help reduce stress and improve the quality of our lives.

Many of us spend all our time living in our past or fantasizing about our future, neither of which actually exist. We miss out on the one true experience of our lives, the gift of the present moment. It is the only thing that any of us can really possess in our lifetime. With each moment, with each breath, we have life. If we are breathing, we know we are alive! And when we are aware we are alive, we can find we have so much to celebrate. Sometimes we literally hold our breath. Other times, although we are breathing, we are doing so without any real awareness. If we do not breathe consciously, we are not aware that we are alive.

So often we forget the gifts of our senses. Many of us have been blessed with sight, taste, touch, smell, and hearing, and each one of them gives us so much to enjoy. The gift of sight can be a daily celebration. Even if you are in a small office or a crowded city, you can look at your hand, at a flower, or at the sky. There is beauty all around us, just waiting for us to stop, take a few breaths, and appreciate it.

Some come to look, others to see.

–SHERPA TENSING

Every journey begins with a single step.

–CONFUCIUS

To be fully conscious, we must listen instead of just hear and look instead of just see. Simply by stopping our mind-chatter we can appreciate the abundance around us. By going back to our breath, we can continually re-appreciate the precious present. After all, it is all that any of us really have in this life.

Mindfulness is a practice, not a religion. Living mindfully, with awareness, can actually help make us better Christians, Jews, Buddhists, Muslims, Hindus or followers of whatever spiritual traditions we may have been born into or have chosen for ourselves.

Three Mindful Practices

The basic components of the Mindful Way journey are three daily mindful practices and some weekly mindful exercises. The three daily practices are Mindful Meditation, Mindful Memoirs, and Mindful Gratitudes. These mindful practices are consistent for the duration of this eight-week course. They will take you forty minutes in the morning and five minutes at night. These forty-five minutes every day will be life changing and will help bring you more peace, joy, and freedom.

It will also greatly help your journey if you can form a group to meet weekly for the next eight weeks. Even if this is only one or two other people, having a support group can encourage you to stay on the path for eight weeks. Once a week, meet together and discuss the week's chapter. I guarantee that you will find yourself learning so much more just from listening to another person's viewpoint. And you may wish to follow the Weekly Group Facilitation Guidelines (Appendix A) at the end of this book.

I have always felt that groups are extremely powerful. In a group we realize that we are never truly alone in this life. We realize that

Pay attention to time, it is not yours, only the now.

–UNKNOWN

*When the Student
is ready, the
Teacher will
appear.*

—CONFUCIUS

we are all "inter-beings" experiencing the same feelings and emotions as most other members of a group. In a group we also experience the support and acceptance of what is happening to each one of us in the course of our life's journey.

Groups are truly powerful, because in them we feel we are a community of human beings all traveling down the same river of life together in one large boat. We are no longer swimming or struggling alone in this river of life, but floating down the river together. With a supportive community we will not get exhausted and drown. We are no longer the rock thrown into the river that sinks to the bottom. In a group, we feel like we are a boat full of stones floating on the surface of the river together.

REFLECTION: MY OWN GROUND ZERO

My own journey started over fifteen years ago. At that time, over the course of an eighteen-month period, I suffered ten personal losses. I had experienced the deaths of two of the people I loved most in the world: my eighteen-year-old nephew Thomas and my wonderful father-in-law Bob, killed in traffic accidents exactly six months apart. Others that I loved deeply also died in a short period of time.

But along with these losses, I realized I'd also lost myself. In the past two decades, I had spent most of my time caring for my sick parents, my husband, and my children. I had also spent a lot of time focusing on caring for my business and the people who worked with me. I'd somehow forgotten to care for and know myself.

I guess I really needed a large rear-ender to wake me up. I know that our greatest learning in life comes from adversity, but this was a period of great sorrow and depression for me. What followed this time of trouble was a 366-day backpacking journey all around this beautiful Earth. This introduced me to many different ways of looking at and perceiving my world.

One of the most significant happenings during that year was visiting a number of countries in Asia where Buddhism is practiced as a way of life. It's not only a religion, but a philosophy, a way of being. There was a peace and joy in the people I met that I had never experienced or seen within my own Anglican/Catholic upbringing. I found my greatest teacher, Thich Nhat Hanh, and my journey of awakening truly began. The only advice that my teacher ever gave me personally was three gently spoken words: "Practice well, Jeanie." I have tried very hard to do this over the years, and when I remember to practice being mindful, I find it can work miracles in my life. I have shared these teachings both in Vancouver, Canada and on the islands of Bermuda. With my husband John, I have founded two Mindfulness Practice Communities for anyone interested in overcoming daily suffering. I write a weekly column on the practice of mindfulness for a newspaper.

Before my losses and my journey, if someone had asked me what I wanted to do with my life, I would have fumbled for an answer. Now, I can express it in one simple sentence: I want to assist people in having more peace, joy, and freedom in the precious present. Of course there are no quick fixes in life and without action and practice nothing will actually change for

The present is always more accessible than the past. In fact that's all there is really.

–GERRY FEWSTER

us. But my own experience with great loss has taught me that when you learn to live with moment-by-moment awareness, your life will start to change in so many ways.

Mindful Meditation

Using meditation, we can stop our minds from dwelling in the past or fantasizing about the future, and we learn how to re-appreciate and celebrate the precious present. The key is to meditate for ten to twenty minutes every morning, immediately after you get out of bed. Just do it—the results will surprise you.

Every morning set your alarm forty-five minutes early and get up for your Mindful Meditation. Many of us feel that we already do not get enough sleep and so you might have some resistance to waking up even earlier. But you will find that getting up forty-five minutes earlier to meditate will actually give you more energy rather than less! And remember, you are doing this for you, and there can be no change in your life without action.

Many years ago, a very lovely French monk named Thay Doji, a student of Thich Nhat Hanh, taught me how to meditate. Start by finding a comfortable space and a place to sit (a corner of your bedroom, the living room, even the kitchen or the bathroom will work if you have a comfortable sitting spot). You may use a cushion or a stool, or you may just sit in an upright chair with your feet placed flat on the ground. Either way, the point is to have the feeling of a strong back and a soft belly, and to keep your head erect and neck straight. Sit in such a way that your body is com-

A person who thinks all the time has nothing to think about except thoughts, so he loses touch with reality and lives in a world of illusion.

—ALAN WATTS

fortable and relaxed, but not slouching. You want to be in a position that you can sit in for ten to twenty minutes. Every day this sitting will get easier.

You may want to keep a timer close by so you know when ten to twenty minutes have passed. Next, close your eyes. Keep them closed for the ten to twenty minutes and follow your breath. Be aware of your breath as it enters and leaves your body. You can say silently, "Breathing in, I know I am breathing in. Breathing out, I know I am breathing out." This is something very simple, but the results are very great. Conscious breathing brings our mind back to our body; we come back to ourselves and peace and ease are reestablished. If you become distracted during the exercise, just bring your awareness gently back to your breath. Our breathing is always with us, a friend to take refuge in. No matter what is going on in our body and our mind, we can always return to our breathing to collect and anchor ourselves. When we are nourished in this way, we are able to be in touch with life in the present moment, with what is going on inside us and around us.

Another way of thinking about following your breath is to imagine a newborn baby lying on a blanket in front of you, and to breathe the same way that she would. A baby breathes only with her tummy; there is no upper chest or rib area breathing. Try using this method for your fifteen minutes of Mindful Meditation every morning. Never force your breath. If you notice your breathing is shallow, just being aware of that fact will help it to relax and it will naturally grow deeper and slower as well as lighter in quality. Your breathing should be light and natural and should not be audible. Focusing on breathing this way may be a little difficult at first, but after a week or so you will find it becoming more of a habit. You may also find that using this conscious breathing calms

Learn to get in touch with the silence within yourself and know that everything in this life has a purpose.

–ELISABETH KUBLER-ROSS

*Seek not outside
yourself,
heaven is within.*

–MARY LOU COOK

you throughout the day, even when you are not meditating, especially if you have just become upset.

The word "meditation" may seem too foreign or too religious for you. However, we all have practiced meditation at some point in our daily lives. You can see babies meditating all the time, as they stare for hours at a ceiling fan or the way the light plays across a wall. When you sit down in a chair to relax and your mind stops thinking about the day's activities for a few minutes, you are already meditating. When you watch a sunset and you really see the sunset, that is a meditation.

You may have other negative ideas that would get in the way of your meditating every morning—perhaps you're afraid you'll go crazy sitting still or feel you can't possibly "waste" ten to twenty minutes just sitting. Here are some of the positives about meditation that you can repeat to yourself (or even tape to your alarm clock) to keep you on track:

- Sitting every day will calm me down.
- My family and friends will support me.
- I can stop my mind for 10/20/30/60 seconds.
- I can learn to breathe like a baby.
- My thoughts come and go as I sit.
- I do have the time to meditate.
- Sitting helps me become more peaceful and calm.
- I seek out or create a community to support me.
- I can set the alarm forty-five minutes early.
- Meditation is going to change my life.

Mindful Memoirs

Mindful Memoirs are designed to help you have a greater under-standing and acceptance of yourself. Every morning, immediately after your meditation, write a minimum of two pages. Specific Mindful Memoirs exercises are listed at the end of each chapter or you can write about your positive and negative feelings about the morning meditation. Do not stop writing and do not reread.

Each of these Mindful Memoir exercises can inspire two to four pages of writing. Take a pen and lined paper and just write. If you get stuck and cannot think what to write, just write anything that comes into your mind—even if it is "I can't think of anything to write!"—until the next thought comes along. But do not stop writ-ing! Maintain an uninterrupted flow of writing. This allows your inner voice to speak to you, without your mind interfering. Con-tinue to write until you have completed a minimum of two pages. Soon, you may find yourself able to write up to three or four pages.

Keep these pages in a three-ring binder or a file folder or a large envelope. You may use your computer, but I have found that hand-written memoirs are much better. The flow of unconscious energy pours more easily onto the paper when we use a pen rather than a computer keyboard. Maybe it has something to do with the fact that when you use a computer, you're putting a machine in between your unconscious thoughts and their expression.

The main reason for writing Mindful Memoirs is simple: this writing will help you begin to understand yourself in a deeper way, because it forces you to look deeply into your life. You can then begin to understand your thought patterns, why you react to peo-ple and situations, and to become more aware of the judgments your mind makes. When you understand yourself better you can

The longest journey is the journey inward.

–DAG HAMMARSKJOLD

begin to love yourself. Then you begin to understand and love others for themselves. So just let your writing flow! After all, understanding ourselves is the first step to understanding and accepting life and others.

Mindful Gratitude

One of the ways that I find essential in trying to lead a more mindful life is to express my gratitude daily. Every night, before I go to sleep, the very last conscious thought is my Gratitude List. Go out and treat yourself to a beautiful little journal or notebook. Then, every night, write five Mindful Gratitudes in this book. If your mind goes blank, you can start with this gratitude: "I am thankful for my breath/life." Another gratitude will follow.

I find that writing about what I am grateful for leads me to greater mindfulness, because when I am grateful for what I have—rather than what I want or don't have—I am so much more accepting of what is. Accepting what is and being grateful for what is happening in the moment is actually mindfulness or total awareness. Therefore when I write about what I am grateful for, I am actually being totally present to my feelings. Mindfulness is totally about awareness of body, feelings, mind, and perceptions. Writing about a previous "present moment" later in a Gratitude and appreciating it again helps me fully appreciate the Now.

Always my first gratitude each night is, "Today I am grateful for my life (or for my breath, without which I am not alive)." Then I usually add a couple of personal attributes such as: "Today I am grateful for my enthusiasm." " Today I am grateful for my creativity." "Today I am grateful for my sense of humor." Then I add any events that that stuck with me, for example, "Today I am grateful-

Gratitude unlocks the fullness of life. It turns what we have into enough, and more. It turns denial into acceptance, chaos to order, and confusion to clarity. It can turn a meal into a feast, a house into a home, a stranger into a friend. Gratitude makes sense of our past, brings peace for today, and creates a vision for tomorrow.

–MELODY BEATTIE

for spending time with my daughter Larissa." "Today I am grateful for a cup of tea with my friend Bonnie." Once you start, you may find it hard to stop at just five gratitudes.

REFLECTION: THANK YOU SO VERY MUCH

For twenty-five years I had a beloved Northern Irish father-in-law, named Bob. Ten years ago he was killed in a car accident. Bob was a very simple-living, quiet gentleman—a hard-working man whose first love was his wife and his family, then his ability to sing in his church choir, and then the country of his birth. Although Northern Ireland has been, and still is, a country torn apart by sectarian violence, Bob was one of the most tolerant and accepting people I have met in my life. Whenever Bob received anything he always said, "Thank you, thank you so very much."

When I first knew him, I have to admit that the endless repetitions of "thank you" bothered me a little. But over the years I grew to understand more fully where he was coming from. He was an aware and mindful man, just pleased with what he had in that moment. His way of expressing gratitude helped to raise others' consciousness, well-being, and happiness. It gave others around him much peace in every moment. As my youngest son, Tim, said after Bob was killed, "Grandpa was a superstar."

It is we who are the creators of joy and magic, sorrow and peace in our lives. I truly believe that being mindfully

Travel is fatal to prejudice, bigotry, and narrow-mindedness and many of our people need it sorely on these accounts.

–MARK TWAIN

grateful is a way of allowing our life to flow, rather than letting events get in the way and cause us much grief and unhappiness.

Mindful Exercises

Each week there will be mindful exercises for you to try. Read and review these exercises at the beginning of the week. Commit to doing one or two of them, or more if possible. They will promote self-reflection and will unlock a great amount of self-knowledge.

- Write a short description of how your life has been for the last ten years. However, do it as if you were living in the future—ten years from your present age.
- One day this week eat a meal in silence. That means no TV, no reading, no conversation with others. Just enjoy eating for the sake of enjoying the food.
- One day this week go for a half-hour walk and start the practice of walking meditation. For a full explanation of walking meditation, see Appendix D.
- At the end of the week, write down any issues that have come up over the week that you may like to look at more deeply with your Mindful Way group.

REFLECTION:
HURRICANES CAN CHANGE COURSE

It was to be the first hurricane experience of my lifetime.
I was alone at home in Bermuda, as my husband was away
"off island." I was excited, but also scared of the unknown.
Hurricane Erin was the first hurricane of the 2001 season to
threaten Bermuda. The government had issued hurricane
preparation warnings and set up a shelter for those in need.
The police had come by my home with a warning and the
supermarkets were crazy with islanders stocking up on food.
The local newspapers, the Internet, TV, and radio stations were
giving hour by hour reports on Erin's increasing power and
steady progress towards our island home. To make things more
confusing, the time she was due to hit kept changing. I had
bought plenty of food, bottled water, a flashlight, and batter-
ies for the radio. I filled the bathtub with water, closed and
locked all the windows and doors, and moved the potted
plants and garden furniture inside, all well in advance of the
hurricane's ever changing "hit" time. Then I sat and waited.

As I waited, my mind went into overdrive. My imagination
saw huge waves crashing over our dock and the sea washing
into our living room. The winds were wild and horrendous,
and of course, the electricity and all communications went out
for days. The island airport had to be closed and I wouldn't see
my husband, who had been away for six weeks, for another
few days. I was upset and sad. The cleanup would take hundreds of hours of work and the destruction to property would

*To travel hopefully
is a better thing
than to arrive.*

–ROBERT LOUIS STEVENSON

*It is one of the
most beautiful
compensations
of life that no man
can sincerely try
to help another
without helping
himself.*

–RALPH WALDO EMERSON

run in the millions. As it turned out, these were nothing more than the projections of my mind because, in the end, Erin never visited Bermuda. Aside from the necessary physical preparation, my emotional worry was a total waste of energy. During that time of worry I had completely ignored the possibility of living in the present moment.

When disaster does strike, it's important that we do focus on it, being present with the tragedy and giving it all our attention and resources, instead of just turning away because it is too much to bear. I visited Sri Lanka after the tsunami in December 2004 and the devastation to that country was dreadful. The heartbreak and suffering of the people felt overwhelming. It was staying present and noticing the courage of the survivors and the support of all their fellow citizens that allowed me to begin to absorb the depth of what had happened. My own son Timothy was supposed to have been in Sri Lanka at the time and had changed his plans at the last minute. Similarly, when Hurricane Katrina struck the southern U.S. in 2005, it reminded me of how critically important it is that communities have all the resources they need and are thoroughly prepared for natural disasters such as hurricanes. Without proper focus and attention in New Orleans, the tragedy was exacerbated in more ways than most of us could ever imagine.

But with Hurricane Erin, I was living in an imagined future. There was no way that my worrying was helping anyone actually in need of help. As I sat and waited, miserable and worrying, I missed out on enjoying a walk along the beautiful South Shore beaches to watch the waves. I didn't really hear the beautiful music playing on our CD player. I didn't even remember eating my dinner, let alone tasting and appreciating the delicious food. My greatest enemy, forgetfulness, had taken over. I had forgotten to be mindful and enjoy the present moment.

Later, I learned that one of the reasons Erin hadn't hit Bermuda was because she had become stronger and veered off in a different direction. I realized that when my imagination and my thoughts became stronger, I could have done the same thing. Instead of projecting into a future that hadn't arrived, I could have changed the course of my thinking and imagination, and come back to mindfully enjoying the present moment. We all have the ability to stop, breathe, and change the direction of our thinking. After all, the present moment is the only place to find real peace and joy.

Mindful Memoirs

Every morning take a pen and lined paper and just write for two to four pages. If you get stuck and cannot think what to write, just write anything that comes into your mind until the next thought comes along. Do not stop writing. This is very important. Again, the main reason for doing this is that the deeper you look at yourself, the better you begin to understand what really makes you tick. You can then begin to understand your thought patterns, why you react to people and situations, and the judgments you make. When you understand yourself better, you can begin to love yourself, and

Knock and the door shall open.

–THE BIBLE

not kill yourself with your own thinking. Your mind can be your greatest enemy.

Weekly Check-in

Be kind, compassionate, accepting, and honest with yourself.

- How many days did I do Mindful Meditation?
- How many days did I do Mindful Memoirs?
- How many nights did I do Mindful Gratitudes?
- How many Mindful Exercises did I do?

NOW

LIKE THE HIBISCUS

GONE BY EVENING

Compassion and Nonviolence

The Five Mindfulness Trainings

Over two thousand years ago, the Buddha offered his students the Five Mindfulness Trainings. The Buddha established these specific practices to help his disciples live more peacefully. All the great spiritual leaders who have walked this Earth have taught the same ideas, but with different words, parables, or stories. Practicing with the Five Mindfulness Trainings as guidelines can help you become calmer and more focused, bringing enlightenment and insight into your life.

Weeks two through six of *A Mindful Way* are focused on studying, practicing, and living these trainings.

The Five Mindfulness Trainings are guidelines rather than commandments. They are not an external ideal imposed by an outside authority, but a gentle guide to watering the fruits of our own awareness. They are the essence of this book, the basis of living a life mindfully.

In talking about the motivation for living by the Five Mindfulness Trainings, Thich Nhat Hanh says:

I shall become a master of this art only after a great deal of practice.

–ERICH FROMM

21

COMPASSION AND NONVIOLENCE

Taking a new step,
uttering a new
word is what peo-
ple fear most.

–FYODOR DOSTOEVSKY

We all suffer in our lives. Some of the effects of this suf-fering are the direct result of alcoholism, drug abuse, sexual abuse or similar behaviors that have been passed down from generation to generation. There is a deep malaise in today's society. When we put young persons into society without trying to protect them, they receive violence, hatred, fear, and insecurity every day, and eventually they become sick. Our conversa-tions, TV programs, advertisements, newspapers, and magazines all water the seeds of suffering in young people and not–so–young people. We feel a kind of vac-uum in ourselves and try to fill it by overeating, exces-sively reading, mindlessly talking, smoking, drinking, watching TV, going to the movies, consuming and acquiring "stuff," and even overworking. When we take sanctuary in these things it only makes us feel hungri-er and far less satisfied, so we need some preventive medication to protect ourselves and make us healthy again. We have to find a cure for our illness and find something that is good, beautiful, and true.

The Five Mindfulness Trainings are the cure for this malaise, and are love expressed by attentiveness, awareness, and insight. To love is to understand, protect, and bring well–being to the object of our love. When we are aware, conscious, or mindful, we can see that by refraining from doing "this," we prevent "that" from happening. The Buddha said: this is because that is. There is no this without that.

The Five Mindfulness Trainings are a mirror to help us identify who we are truly are. Just as when we look into a mirror we see an image of ourselves reflected back, when we practice the Five Mindfulness Trainings we see a deeper understanding of ourselves reflected back to us. But they don't only teach us about ourselves; they can also help deepen our experience of community. They not only protect us, but others too. We see that our so-called individual self, our "I," is tied in with all others. These trainings allow us to look at our lives, taking responsibility firstly for ourselves and then for others. These trainings help us first to take care of ourselves, then our local community, and then our world. They help us experiment and experience the truth, the truth about our own journey through this life. By following just one of these trainings, our own lives will transform and give us confidence to approach almost any situation. They allow us to put our personal lives and spiritual lives in order and to act with wisdom and compassion.

The First Mindfulness Training

Aware of the suffering caused by the destruction of life,
I am committed to cultivating compassion and learning ways
to protect the lives of people, animals, plants, and minerals.
I am determined not to kill, not to let others kill, and not to support
any act of killing in the world, in my thinking, and in my way of life.

Practicing the Trainings

Each of the Five Mindfulness Trainings begins with the words, "Aware of the suffering caused by..." This is an extremely important aspect of these trainings, for until you are aware that you are suffering, you cannot do anything to change it. You can go on, day in and day out, killing yourself with your own thoughts and your way of living.

You create your life
with each choice
you make.

–UNKNOWN

Have you ever been angry with someone or something? Have you ever been obsessed about something or someone in your life? We spend nearly eighty percent of every day re-thinking the same thoughts that we thought yesterday! Thinking is the base of everything that happens in our lives. To create happiness in your life, it is vitally important that you first become aware of your thoughts. For this, you have to use your concentration.

If you start to look at your thoughts as if they are simply passing ideas, you can look at them more objectively. Like everything else in life, your thoughts are impermanent and therefore are subject to constant change. You have to remember that without correct understanding of a situation or a person, your thoughts can be misleading and can create confusion, anger, or hatred. That is why it is so important to develop correct insight. So, first you have to be aware, and then use your concentration to understand, and then use your insights to change your thoughts. In other words, understanding lets us change violent thinking into nonviolent thoughts.

To practice this nonviolence in your life, you have to first learn how to deal peacefully with yourself. If you are able to create true harmony within yourself, then you will know how to deal with family, friends, and associates. If you realize that we are all of the one creation, of the one divinity, of the one universe, then you can see the nature of our oneness (or our "interbeing") and you can stop your blaming.

No matter how committed to nonviolence we are, we all feel angry, frustrated, and even violent sometimes. We need to find someone who is willing to listen to us, someone who is capable of understanding our suffering. In each of us, there are seeds of a certain amount of violence and a certain amount of nonviolence. You can make the decision to be less violent with your own thoughts and cultivate compassion in yourself. This is an effective beginning towards changing your life. Our minds can never be completely free of anger and violence. But the First Mindfulness Training can be our North Star, our guide toward nonviolence. Even though you know that it is impossible to actually reach the North Star, you can proceed in that direction.

Another way to develop insight is to choose to stop blaming and arguing. Even if we are blaming those who support war, when we argue for peace but do so in a violent way, we are co-responsible for violence in the world.

Understanding how our actions are linked with all the other actions in the world is the key to compassion and love. With such an insight we can see clearly and help our own governments to see more clearly. Rather than condemning others, we can say, "This [war, policy, etc.] is unjust, destructive, and not worthy of us."

So to practice nonviolence we must first look within ourselves. We can't divide nonviolence and violence into two unrelated camps. Not only is this inaccurate, but it only leads to more violence. If we want to have a real impact on the level of violence in the world, we will need to work with like-minded people as well as with those whom we would otherwise condemn. Some of us were raised with the edict to "love our neighbors, as ourselves," but this is very challenging in practice!

The first thing we can do is to commit to being a living embodiment of nonviolence. To practice nonviolence, we need to first be gentle towards ourselves. We need to practice loving kindness and compassion towards our body and feelings. With mindfulness, we can begin to transform the wars within our own body and feelings. One of the techniques for doing this is conscious breathing.

My daily meditations nourish my body and my soul, and they honor the presence of God within me.

– UNKNOWN

Whenever we are angry or upset, we can stop what we are doing and not say anything. Then, breathe in and out several times, aware of each in–breath and each out–breath. If we continue to feel upset we can go for a mindful walking meditation, aware of each slow step and each breath we take. By cultivating peace within ourselves, we bring about peace in society. Peace depends on you. So in the end, this First Mindfulness Training is really about developing kindness and compassion within yourself.

REFLECTION:
SLOW DOWN AND ENJOY THE RIDE

*A mind too active
is no mind at all.*

–THEODORE ROETHKE

All major religions have some version of the precept: "Thou shall not kill." When we think of this precept, many of us imagine guns. But I am personally aware of the suffering caused by one of the most lethal weapons many people possess: a car. My eighteen-year-old nephew Thomas and my healthy and extremely active father-in-law Bob were both killed by moving vehicles. Thomas was riding his bicycle and was hit by a truck and thrown to the curbside where he sustained a fatal injury. Bob was killed as the passenger in a car driven by a friend at a busy intersection just as dusk was descending. Their deaths were caused by simple mindless errors. The suffering caused by just one second of unawareness or non-conscious driving has been immense for my family.

Where I live in Bermuda, we have the pleasure of having a top speed limit of twenty-one miles per hour. It's unnecessary to speed on this small island. Each time we find ourselves speeding, even if we are late for something important, we can ask ourselves: "Am I more interested in the destination or in the journey?" After all, we are all headed for the same destination in life; death will not pass any of us by. The only time we can be alive is when we enjoy the journey and the present moment!

The United Kingdom Department of Transport once did a study of long distance car trips. One group of people drove only at the legal speed limit, while another group drove at well over the speed limit. The results were amazing. Over a distance of a few hundred miles, they found there was very little difference in the length of time it took for both groups to arrive at the same destination. However, the group that drove within the speed limit enjoyed their journey, while the other group reported feeling much more stressed.

It is quite common for people to drive and talk on their cell phones at the same time, even though this is exceedingly dangerous. Living in awareness requires that you do not intentionally do two things at once: uni-tasking instead of multi-tasking. Either you drive or you stop and talk on the telephone. As of 2006, thirty-one countries have changed their driving laws to reflect the increased number of accidents occurring while using a hand-held device. In these countries it is now illegal to use a hand-held cell phone while driving. People pride themselves on their sophisticated communication devices, but real communication is not produced by this modern technology. Trying to talk and drive at the same time is like trying to

What lies behind us and what lies before us are tiny matters compared to what lies within us.

–RALPH WALDO EMERSON

The center that I cannot find is known to my unconscious mind.

–W. H. AUDEN

There is nothing either good or bad, but thinking makes it so.

–HAMLET, ACT II, SCENE 2

The day is ending and our life is one day shorter. Let us look carefully at what we have done. Let us practice diligently, putting our whole heart into the practice of mindfulness. Let us live deeply each moment in freedom, so that time doesn't slip away meaninglessly.

–THICH NHAT HANH

eat a meal and watch the TV at the same time; you cannot do or enjoy either fully.

The mindful teaching here is simple: when you sit you sit, when you walk you walk, when you talk you talk, and when you drive you drive! Perhaps this way of living seems boring or too simple at first, but you'll find there is a wealth of stimulation in the present moment, if you just allow yourself to notice it. When you become really alive and awakened to the precious present, everything you do or touch feels like a miracle.

Watering the Seeds of Peace

As we look into the practice of this First Mindfulness Training, we know that when we buy or consume something we may be condoning some form of killing. While practicing the protection of people, animals, plants, and minerals we know that we are also protecting ourselves. We then feel in loving touch with all species on Earth. However, feeling loving kindness or compassion is not really enough; we have to learn how to express it. Love goes together with understanding and insight to show us how to act. However, our greatest enemy is forgetfulness, forgetting to be totally aware.

If you look after a plant it will become healthy and lush. In the same way, we have to care for our own life by watering ourselves daily with compassion and self-care, in order to prevent ourselves from becoming hard and shriveled up. We can bloom like a beautiful flower, as long as we nourish our mindfulness daily. By watering the seeds of peace in ourselves and those around us, we will become alive and realize peace and compassion in the world.

To water the seeds of peace in ourselves, we begin by bringing peace into our body, and this also brings peace into our mind. You may like to do the following exercise when you sit in meditation. Follow your breathing and become one with your breath. Once your breathing is calm you can practice, "Breathing in, I am aware of my whole body. Breathing out, I am aware of my whole body." When you have practiced like this for some time, continue with, "Breathing in, I make my whole body calm and at peace. Breathing out, I make my whole body calm and at peace." Sitting like this even for a few minutes relaxes and calms body and mind and allows you to let go of preoccupations. You can continue with, "Breathing in, I am making my mind happy and at peace. Breathing out, I am making my mind happy and at peace." Sitting in this way, joy and peace begin to permeate and nourish your body and mind. Sitting like this for a few minutes each day will bring peace into your relationships and your daily life.

You may want to add some exercises that put you in touch with the wonders of life and with what is good in your life in order to cultivate a feeling of joy and well-being and counteract our tendency to dwell on what is not right. For example, "Breathing in, I am aware of my two eyes, still in good health. Breathing out, I know that I have two able hands". "In touch with the air, I breathe in. In touch with the sky, I breathe out." "In touch with the trees, I breathe in, in touch with the children, I breathe out." We can nourish ourselves daily with exercises such as these and cultivate our awareness and peace.

The word "enthusiasm" comes from Greek, meaning "filled with God." When you tap into these positive seeds that are within all of

"Would you tell me, please, which way I ought to go from here?"

"That depends a good deal on where you want to get to."

"I don't much care where."

"Then it doesn't matter which way you go,"

"... so long as I get somewhere."

"Oh, you're sure to do that, if only you walk long enough."

–ALICE IN WONDERLAND

us, your life can change. Enthusiasm is actually a spiritual commit-ment, a true loving surrender to all that is around you and with-in you. It is a recognition of all that is in creation, including people, animals, plants, and minerals. Just like two snowflakes, no two of us have been created the same. The practice of the First Mindful-ness Training is a celebration of reverence for life. When you are enthusiastic about the beauty of life, you begin to do everything in your power to protect it.

REFLECTION: MINDFUL ACTION

One day, our telephone line at home had been affected by a storm that hit Bermuda. The static had become so bad that we could not even hear ourselves think while on the phone, let alone hear those who were calling us! I called the telephone company and was told by customer service that someone would come by to fix the problem in five to seven working days. Island living can be quite slow-paced! We went off-island for a short vacation, leaving a friend in the house with a note that the phone company person would be com-ing by. When we returned two weeks later, our friend report-ed that the telephone company hadn't come by or called.

I was upset, because I thought the problem would be solved while I was gone, so I called again, only to be told by the cus-tomer service representative that there was no record of my request made nearly two weeks earlier! I was now angry and upset, because I felt I was being accused of not telling the truth.

My initial reaction was to yell and scream. Instead, I followed my breathing and went out for an hour of walking meditation. When I'd calmed down, I wrote a letter to the phone company. The letter didn't blame them; it just stated how I felt. Just coming back to the present moment and truly expressing my feelings, I felt more at peace. My anger, like ice, melted into a pool of water.

The person who received my letter read it mindfully and understood. People from the Bermuda Telephone Company called or visited us every day for the next four days! By the end of the week a new line had been installed. I was so grateful for the First Mindfulness Training that had given me guidance for dealing with this small frustration. While this example wasn't a severe or life-threatening situation, the Five Mindfulness Trainings offer us a path of calm and clarity to follow in situations both large and small.

When you are truly alive to the present moment, everything you do or touch is a miracle. Practicing mindfulness is to return to life in the present moment. The practice of the First Mindfulness Training is actually a celebration of the reverence for life, compassion, and generosity. When we do everything in our power to protect ourselves and all of life, miracles do happen.

Mindful Exercises

- This is an exercise I learned from Jack Kornfield, a Buddhist teacher and author of *A Path With Heart*. It will help you to start experiencing joy and peace in your life. This week, purposely bring no harm in thought, word, or deed to any living creature. Become aware of any living beings in your world that you normally ignore and cultivate a sense of care and reverence for them. Acknowledge an associate's smile or another's kind words on the phone. Appreciate the blue sky and sea or the coloring on a stray cat. Really listen to the birds singing or the whispering of the trees.

- Start a Mindfulness Life Collage. Ask yourself what you really need in your life to experience joy and peace. Go through magazines and cut out pictures, images, or quotes to which you are attracted. It may be about your ideal environment, your ideal job/career, your ideal partnership, your ideal community, or your ideal way of living. While you are doing this, ask yourself how you can create a kinder life for yourself.

- Go to your closet and donate or pass on six outfits that you have not worn in a year or six things that you haven't used in your home. This will start to create space for what you really need in your life: loving kindness and compassion.

- Every time you say to yourself "I should" or "I can't," replace it with a positive thought, such as "I could" or "I can." When we get rid of the "shoulds" and "can'ts" we start to focus on the positive aspects of what we can or could do in our lives.

- Buy a bag of mixed beads from a craft shop. Every time you make a judgment about someone or something, take a bead and put it in an empty glass. At the end of each day, count the number of beads in the glass. Write down the number and do this exercise daily for a week. The object of this exercise is to attempt to have an empty glass at the end of each day and to think about how often you are being unkind or uncompassionate to others.

REFLECTION: A REVERENCE FOR ALL LIFE

One week, my article for the *Bermuda Royal Gazette* newspaper was trapped inside my very sick computer. Without paying attention, I had opened an email that said, "I have a very special screen saver for you," only to discover that the email contained a terrible virus. All of a sudden my computer started to reproduce the same email to my list of contacts and I just couldn't stop it! I breathed and unplugged my laptop. But it continued to produce virus-infected emails! I couldn't even stop it by shutting off the power. The result was that my computer had to go to the hospital.

At the computer hospital, I had a conversation with the technician working there. I asked him where these viruses are born. "Anywhere in the world," he told me. We then talked about why people make them. Was it greed, hatred, anger, or maybe the desire for a day of fame in a computer magazine? I contemplated the interconnectedness of our world. If you

33

The mind grows by what it feeds on.

–J.G. HOLLAND

are not there, then I am not here. Because of what someone thousands of miles away had felt and acted on, I was at the hospital with my sick computer, talking to this very nice computer guy.

Mindful Memoirs: Birth to Age Seven

In Week One, the idea behind Mindful Memoirs was to write continuously about any thoughts that came into your mind. The main reason for doing this was that the deeper you look at yourself, the better you begin to understand yourself. You can then begin to understand your thought patterns, why you react to people and situations and the judgments you make. When you understand yourself better, you can begin to love yourself and not kill yourself with your own thinking—our minds can be our greatest enemy.

This week, take any one of the following ideas and write about them daily when doing your Mindful Memoirs. Write three or four pages. Use this list of ideas to trigger deeper thoughts and memories. Take a pen and lined paper and just write. Do not stop writing. Ignore your brain and just let your inner voice speak to you.

- What details of your birth do you know? The place, your weight, the hour, were your parents expecting a boy or girl, where was your father, who was told first, were you born under unusual circumstances, in a hospital, at home, etc.?
- How were you named? Do you like your name? What were your parents' names, your grandparents' names, and

other immediate birth or adopted family members' names? Write a little about each of them. Maybe write why each person was called by that name and how you feel about his or her name. Write down the main personality traits, values, and gifts that you remember about these relatives. Which one influenced you the most?

- How many children are in your family? Write about your birth order and how it may or may not have affected you.

- How old were your parents when you were born? What did they do for a living at that time? Are there any mementos of your birth?

- What religious or cultural traditions were followed after your birth, if any?

- What games and toys did you play with as a young child? What did you like best about your toys?

- Describe where you lived and what it was like. If you lived in more than one place, describe them all.

- How did your parents describe you as a baby/child? What stories did they tell?

- How did your parents treat you as a baby/child? In what way was love shown to you as a child?

- Did you attend nursery school? What was this experience like?

- Did you have any accidents or illnesses as a baby/child? Were you ever in the hospital? How did these experiences make you feel?

- Did you have family pets growing up? Write about how you felt towards your pet(s) or about a pet you always wanted to have.

- Describe two of your favorite family trips or holidays.
- Write about how you amused yourself as a young child.
- Tell two stories about what you found funny and what scared you as a child.
- Write about your friends at that time and what they were like. Did you have a best friend? Did you have an imaginary friend?
- Describe the most significant event that happened to you between birth and seven years.
- Write about your first memory.
- Write about the smells and foods that you remember from this period.
- What were some of the things happening in the world or in your country at the time of your childhood that affected you or that you remember?

Weekly Check-in

Be kind, compassionate, accepting, and honest with yourself.

- How many days did I do Mindful Meditation?
- How many days did I do Mindful Memoirs?
- How many nights did I do Mindful Gratitudes?
- How many Mindful Exercises did I do?

EACH DAY

LIKE A BLANK PIECE OF PAPER

AWAITS ME

W · E · E · K   T · H · R · E · E

Defeating Oppression

The Second Mindfulness Training

Aware of the suffering caused by exploitation, social injustice, stealing, and oppression, I am committed to cultivating loving kindness and learning ways to work for the well-being of people, animals, plants, and minerals. I will practice generosity by sharing my time, energy, and material resources with those who are in real need. I am determined not to steal and not to possess anything that should belong to others. I will respect the property of others, but I will prevent others from profiting from human suffering or the suffering of other species on Earth."

Oppression, as defined in Webster's dictionary is 1) the unjustly harsh exercise of authority or power, 2) the act or an instance of oppressing, or 3) the feeling of being oppressed in mind or body.

I grew up in the United Kingdom during the very conservative and restricting 1950s. When, in the 1960s and '70s, I connected with the feminist, anti–racism, and antiwar movements, I was surprised by how liberated and joyful I could feel. Now, my life feels somewhere in between. In some ways, I still have serious responsibili-

*It is more blessed
to give than
to receive.*

−ACTS 10:35

ties and respond to social restrictions. In other ways, having the blessing of being retired, I feel rather free. Our social systems, governments, cultures, and even sometimes our own families still act in ways that are very oppressive. But a lot of my own anger has transformed into compassion. Practicing loving kindness seems the most effective way for me to help all people overcome oppression.

There are "big" oppressions that society imposes on us and there are "little" oppressions that many of us feel everyday. Here is one small example of how I used the Second Mindfulness Training to find a way to relieve some personal suffering, without causing any further harm to either myself or the other person. I've always liked doing my shopping at smaller local stores. I like the village and community feeling that comes from knowing the people in a store and having a relationship beyond just the transaction. However, I also find myself getting impatient when I am in a hurry and the shop owner is doing something else or seems to be ignoring me. I feel powerless and frustrated; what can I do? The first thing is I return to my breath. I notice how frustrated I am and wait for those feelings to subside. When they do, I can notice the other person. What are they doing? Are they feeling busy, overworked, bored? I can also think about how to express my need for help. I might say something like, "I need to ask for something. Could you please help me?" Instead of blaming and criticizing the other person, I can still express what I need to express and get my needs met without stealing the other person's peace.

Sometimes I become the oppressor of others. I have privileges of class and race that are impossible to forget. Throughout my life, inadvertently and without mindfulness, I have sometimes been unaware of these privileges and have hurt others. Other times, I can be forgetful and hurtful with those I love. I can forget to praise my family members for being kind and generous or I forget to give others a genuine compliment on how well they have treated me or for a task well done. I find that the people I am closest to often get the short end of the stick and that strangers benefit more from my remembering. When I do forget, or become suddenly aware of ways in which I am oppressive to others, I understand the importance of acknowledging it and doing what's possible to remedy the situation. I also have learned not to be too hard on myself. With every moment I can begin again.

Generosity

The Second Mindfulness Training asks us not to steal. Implied in this mindfulness training is the idea of generosity. We can ensure that we do not take too much. To live we need animals, plants, and minerals, for we all live in this world and we all share its resources. If we didn't have bees to pollinate our crops for us, we couldn't live. If we didn't have earthworms aerating our soil, we couldn't grow our crops. If we learn to love nature around us, we can be content with whatever we have or whatever we do. To cultivate generosity towards all living beings is a key part of living a spiritual life. However, we have to remember to *practice* generosity. The Buddha said, "I would not let a single meal pass without sharing it in some way," while Jesus taught us to, "Give and you shall receive."

Jack Kornfield talks about three ways to practice generosity. The first is tentative giving, usually of some material resource. We take an object and say to ourselves that we probably do not have any use for it. We think, "Maybe I will give it away." This is an easy way to create joy for ourselves and help another being. It is about sharing and connection.

Assist another, rather than help.

–UNKNOWN

The next level is friendly giving, or helping others to rely upon themselves. It is about sharing our time, our knowledge, our energies, and the material resources we have. We do not need a lot of possessions to be happy. It is the relationships in our lives that determine our happiness or misery. Joy arises in the heart only in relationships.

The third level of giving is the gift of non-fear. It requires giving without fear of losing something, the gift of something precious. With non-fear giving, the gift is our time and energy and we give it to someone happily with the hope that they will enjoy it. Thich Nhat Hanh talks about how our own understanding and lack of fear about death or loss can be of great value to those who are dying, suffering, or in difficulty. Folk are afraid of many things: we are insecure, fearful of being alone, fearful of sickness and dying. To help others with these fears is to practice the third kind of gift giving.

The Second Mindfulness Training is a very deep practice. It is about time, energy, and material resources. Time is for being with others, being with someone who is sick or dying, or suffering in some other way. We all suffer daily in many small ways. Truly being with a person for only five minutes is a true gift—especially if it involves deep listening. The gift of time is a gift that allows us to give of ourselves deeply and to share all we have with others.

If you practice generosity—whether it is giving your time, energy, goods, or money—not to please your self-image or an external authority, but just because you want to, you will find that you become more peaceful and content. You do not have to give everything away—remember to always first be compassionate and kind to your self. However, this kind of open kindness and generosity is very special. In giving of yourself, you will receive far more in return.

REFLECTION: A BERMUDA ROSE

Bermuda is one of the most beautiful places on this Earth to be, full of colorful flowers. As someone who came to this island as an adult, as a guest, I never expected that I would also be so affected by the beautiful Bermudian women I have met.

One of the Bermudian women I've met who has had the greatest impact on me is named Rose. To some of her friends she is Rose, "Rosie-Posie" or just "Posie." Rose has been battling cancer for a number of years, and like so many other women, it started in her breast. I met her at Agape House, Bermuda's cottage hospice where I was working as a volunteer. Rose and I made an immediate heart connection, and her courage, mindfulness, and humility have been an inspiration.

Rose's family was so very special to her. Her father was a hard working shipwright and her mother was, as she puts it, just a homemaker. Her family was one of the first black Bermudian families to own their own home in Somerset. Her mother died when Rose was just sixteen. She thanks God daily that her mother was so nurturing, mindful, understanding, and caring. Her mother's paradigm enabled Rose to be both a sister and a mother to her younger sibling who was only ten at the time of their mother's death. Even today she often asks herself, "What would my mother do or say in this situation?" In the teachings of mindfulness, it is good to be aware that the actions of the present moment are our future. Rose talks fondly of her childhood, about reading stories with her mother and taking picnics on the tiny islands of Bermuda. Her parents were

You give but little when you give of your possessions. It is when you give of yourself that you truly give.

–KAHLIL GIBRAN

*Great thoughts
reduced to practice
become great acts.*

–HAZLITT

always protective of her and proud and supportive of all the things she achieved. They always did things together as a family. There was always a home cooked meal that the whole family sat down to at the same time. This was a time to share tales of their daily activities and events.

Rose was one of the many young black women sent by the Bermudian government, on a scholarship, to the University of Toronto to study. She specialized in child studies and became a schoolteacher. She first attended university there in 1949. She returned again in 1962 to further her studies. One day when she was attending university classes, she arrived at a lecture crying. Her professor spoke with her after class to find out what was troubling her. Rose said that at the guesthouse where she was staying, she was being treated just like a maid. Although she was a paying guest, the landlady was asking her to wait on tables and telling all the other guests, in a loud whispered voice, "to lock their bedroom doors, just in case Rose might steal something from their rooms." It was blatant racism from a woman who probably had never had any previous contact with a person of color. Rose's professor understood her intense distress and told her that she had some friends who had a very large home in a lovely area of Toronto and that she would ask them if they were interested in renting a room to Rose.

That very night she received a phone call from the professor's friends inviting her to dinner to discuss the possibility of sharing their home. When Rose arrived the following Saturday at six o'clock, she was greeted by a woman named Diana, her husband Charles, and their twin daughters. They all shook her hand to greet her and the two little girls, dressed in their long red nightgowns, curtsied to welcome her. The dinner lasted until one o'clock the following morning. During the course of the evening it was decided that Rose would come to stay for a "ten-day tryout" to see if she liked the family. Forty years later, Rose still goes a couple of times a year to visit her best friends in Toronto! She has her own apartment with all of her own possessions in the very same home that she moved into for that "ten-day tryout." Her friends also make a trip annually to visit her in Bermuda.

Rose became the principal of a school for special children in Southampton Parish. This school was for children who were considered slow or who did not fit into the regular school system. In a lot of cases the children were from homes where there was physical, emotional, or mental abuse. Rose designed the school building and she made sure that her office was right in the center of all school activities. Rose brought her practicality, mindfulness, and her loving presence to the children. She would buy shoes and clothes with her own money whenever some of the children were in need. She also made sure that they had training in practical life skills. Each child could prepare a meal, sew on a button, hem a dress or a pair of pants, use a screwdriver, a hammer, or a saw, and balance a bankbook. She also insisted on clean shirts or blouses, ironed pants or skirts, and polished shoes whenever there was a school outing.

Rose is so very proud of her now grown-up students who have been successful in many of Bermuda's top businesses and

*Kind hearts
are the gardens,
Kind thoughts
are the roots,
Kind words are
the blossoms,
Kind deeds
are the fruits.*

–UNKNOWN

Expect your every
need to be met,
Expect the answers
to every problem,
Expect abundance
on every level,
Expect to grow
spiritually.

–EILEEN CADDY

professions. She talks about one of her old students being the employee of the year twice at one of Bermuda's best-known organizations. She feels that she did make an impact on many young and not so fortunate Bermudians' lives by giving them the same understanding, mindfulness, and compassion that her family and friends, like Diana and Charles, had given her many years before. As Rosie contemplates her own mortality, she returns again and again to the valuable lesson of generosity and mindfulness she learned from her family and from those she met out in the world.

Time, Energy, and Material Resources

The Second Mindfulness Training says: "I am determined not to steal and not to possess anything that should belong to others." This is in part because everything on Earth is our shared gift. In the Western world we have less of the world's population and yet we consume the greatest amount of this beautiful Earth's resources. Many of these natural resources come from countries that are ruled by a military government or dictatorship. Western countries set up inequitable trade terms with these countries that cause the people in those countries to suffer. The mindless consumption of natural resources by the West continues to fuel these situations.

As a global village, we have to act in a very different way if we want to stop the murder of innocent folk around the world. When we take a person's life, we take their most precious possession. This second training has a lot to do with the First Mindfulness Training, which tells us not to kill. If we take from others, we are killing them, even if we do not deal the final blow.

As members of countries that take more than their share, we have a responsibility to give back what has been taken from those countries that have less. This is true both in terms of material resources and also in terms of opportunities for skills training, university, and retreat.

Besides the global level, we can look at the "village" level. How do we contribute to our communities? What resources are shared and are they distributed equitably? We can find applications for the Second Mindfulness Training in every aspect of our lives, from our relationships (sharing equally in the work and wealth of our partnership) to our families, our jobs, and our larger communities.

REFLECTION: A BERMUDA CEDAR TREE

There is a man of very large stature, physically, emotionally, mentally, and spiritually as well, whom I have been privileged to know since I came to Bermuda. He has become my friend, mentor, and teacher. His name is Chesley Trott and he reminds me of the Bermuda cedar (Juniperus Bermudiana), one of his favorite trees. He has the strength and solidity of the tree's trunk and the openness and freedom of its branches. Chesley is a wood carver, sculptor, and artist. He is a great family man and superb teacher to many. He is also an accomplished athlete, a supple seventy-four-year-old golfer, and an excellent tennis player. He is a collector of orchids and bromeliads and he communicates with them daily. He has given generously to his Bermudian community and still continues to do so.

Chesley gives in all the ways that Jack Kornfield mentions, but particularly in the third—he gives the gift of non-fear. He offers joy to others in a way that is not characterized by an outer form. It is not based on showing off, because at its source is a heart of love and compassion. Daily he practices giving joy motivated by generosity. Chesley listens very well and gives totally of himself. As a dark-skinned man, he has experienced prejudice and he speaks with no prejudice to anyone. He is always aware of the safety of all the students in his class when they are using their wood carving tools and equipment and he will tell them immediately and with great patience if they are doing something that is risky.

I first met Chesley at his dockyard studio. I walked into his magical overflowing cave of Bermuda cedar, filled with intoxicating aromas, wood chips everywhere on the floor, classical music playing, the best wood carving tools strewn everywhere on the benches and his beautiful rounded abstract-style wood sculptures. In the midst of this exotic cave was Chesley, who greeted me with generous hospitality. He welcomed me into his studio and offered me a small piece of Bermuda cedar. I have now seen him do this many times to all the folk who come to his studio door.

A number of people in Bermuda helped Chesley when he was a young aspiring artist and he in turn has spent years returning those gifts by helping others. His gifts are of time, energy, and knowledge. In return, many other folk have given him small and large pieces of his beloved Bermuda cedar. They find their way into his studio with these gifts. It is then that he creates the images and visions of his mind by carving these pieces of wood into beautiful touchable sculptures.

Even though he is a talented sculptor, I think Chesley's greatest gift is his skillful teaching. He spent years teaching art and since his retirement he continues to teach those who are interested in woodcarving. One of his greatest pleasures for the last thirty years is to spend time weekly at the Westgate Prison teaching the residents there the skills of woodcarving. Chesley gives them far more than wood carving skills. I suspect he gives them his mindfully generous listening skills. This is a gift of kingly giving or the gift of non-fear. He is so open and non-judgmental in his listening and in his speech, that the prisoners would feel no fear in sharing their suffering with him. With his deep listening skills and generous heart, he helps to relieve the suffering of his students in the prison's wood carving classes.

He talks about his sculptures as visual expressions of his hopes, dreams, experiences, and interests. I see his generous actions as expressions of these hopes, dreams, experiences, and interests. He truly follows the practice of generosity by sharing his time, energy, and material resources with those who are in real need. I have been very blessed to have this man come into my life and deepen my understanding of this Second Mindfulness Training.

The same stream of life that runs through the world runs through my veins night and day and dances in rhythmic measures. It is the same life that shoots in joy through the dust of the earth into the numberless blades of grass and breaks into tumultuous waves of flowers.

–RABINDRANATH TAGORE

Mindful Exercises

- How much time do you spend doing things for yourself? Describe what you do. How much time do you spend doing things for others? Describe these activities.

- How much time do you spend ignoring your own needs? Write down the ways you do this.

- Make a list of the top ten things you most enjoy doing. Write down beside each one when you last did any of these things.

- Choose one or two of these "top ten things you most enjoy doing" and do them this week (or at least take a first step towards doing them).

- Find one situation in your present life that you would like to change, write about why you are stuck, and then take a small step towards changing it.

- Write down ten more changes you would like to make for yourself. Then write down beside each one the first step towards making them.

- Write down ten things you would like to do for others, and the first step towards doing them.

- Write down which of the above exercises you have resisted the most and write about your reasons for doing this.

- Find a place in your home and make private a corner for yourself. Create an altar or a spiritual space. This is not necessarily a religious space, but an area where you can put photos of your family, however you define it, and your friends. Maybe add some candles, incense, or flowers. This place is to remind you daily to take care of yourself. It is a way of showing generosity, kindness, and compassion.

- Write out your own prayer or aspiration and use it daily. Post it in a prominent position in your home (the bathroom is a great spot!) or at work.

- Try speaking only of your own needs and feelings, not blaming others, for one week in any situation where you feel an authority figure, co-workers, family, friends, or neighbors are in any way oppressing you. Try being generous first with yourself and then with others in every single situation of oppression that arises. You will already be practicing the Second Mindfulness Training by sharing your energy and time with those who are in real need. We are all in real need of generosity.

Mindful Memoirs: Age Eight to Age Fourteen

Follow one Mindful Memoirs exercise daily from the list below and write two or three pages. Take a pen, lined paper, and just write. If you get stuck and cannot think what to write, just write anything that comes into your mind, even if it is "I am having difficulty with this," or "what a cold morning," until the next memory comes along. Do not stop writing; it is important to allow your inner voice to speak to you rather than your thinking mind.

- What schools did you attend from age eight to fourteen? Write about first days, whether they were happy times, how you got along with others, friends, and teachers; how you traveled to school, school lunches, classes, sports, etc.

- What subjects at school do you remember most vividly? What teachers and school friends influenced you the most and why was that so? How did these affect your future choices? What subjects did or didn't you like? How were your report cards?

■ Do you still have friends from this period of your life? Have you ever met old friends from this period or do you know what friends are doing now in their lives?

■ Was there anything you particularly wanted as a child? What was the most significant gift you received?

■ Who influenced you the most? Or, what was the most significant thing that happened to you between eight and fourteen years?

■ What teams, clubs, organizations, and competitions did you participate in during these years? Were there any groups that you would have liked to participate in but didn't?

■ Write about your religious beliefs and practices at this time.

■ Write about the foods you liked to eat, clothes you liked to wear, music you liked to listen to, and the books you liked to read.

■ Write about what daydreams you had during this time. Also write about your superstitions.

■ What did you do during your school summer holidays?

■ What did your family talk about around the dinner table? What did your family do on weekends?

■ Were you outgoing or shy as a child? Short or tall, overweight or skinny? How did you dress? How did you do at school? How did this affect you?

■ How did you get along with your immediate or close extended family?

■ Write about what you thought you wanted to be when you "grew up."

- Write about a particular birthday party or other celebration you had during this period, or if you never had one, how you felt about that.
- What toys or games did you cherish during these years? What creative or physical activities did you cherish during this time?
- What was going on in your neighborhood, country, and the world during these years?

REFLECTION:
WELCOME TO THE NEIGHBORHOOD

Those of us raised in Christian traditions are probably very familiar with the teaching, "Love thy neighbor, as thyself." Once we were taught this, we were expected to live our lives in this manner and probably hoped to do so. But most of us find it harder to act on this concept of loving others as ourselves than to just carry around the idea in our heads.

When my husband and I were able to retire to Bermuda, we moved to Salt Kettle in Paget Parish. During the 1980s, while we were living in Canada, we had been lucky enough to take a few family vacations on Salt Kettle. We knew from the first time we were there that this was the place in the world we would most like to live. This was even before we knew what a supportive community it would be. One of the biggest blessings I couldn't have anticipated was the kindly neighbor living just across the road from us. Her name is Hazel and for thirty years she's owned a charming little guesthouse.

Know in your heart what your behavior means. Heart thinking needs to change. What is it about me that invites this feedback/criticism? What self do I need to defend? In attacking back—I am attacking part of myself.

–JOAN HALIFAX

When we arrived at our newly rented home, we didn't have even a mug or spoon in our kitchen. So I walked over to Hazel's, where she promptly loaned us far more than we needed. Soon I began to notice that Hazel's guesthouse lawn was always overflowing with guests in the early evenings. Hazel often joined her guests to watch the sunset, usually with some special little treats she had prepared for them.

One evening we were having dinner in our new home when the sound of bagpipes filled the air. Not sure what was happening, I followed the sounds of the music to Hazel's place. Sure enough, on Hazel's lawn was a large group of people with a very handsome and well-groomed older gentleman sitting in the center of this circle of attentive friends. It was his eighty-fifth birthday. Hazel said that for the last fourteen years she had held a birthday party for her friend. He now lived in a nursing home and she enjoyed spoiling him. She told me that when her husband was dying, her old friend had come over every Sunday afternoon to spend a few hours with her very sick husband. She said, "I can never forget that my friend was a very kind gentleman to my husband, and now it is my turn to return his kindness in some small way." She told me, as she looked at me with a very kind and penetrating stare, "The only thing in life we can do, is to be kind." Her words, so simple and direct, struck a chord in my heart and return to me every day.

Weekly Check-in

Be kind, compassionate, accepting, and honest with yourself.

- How many days did I do Mindful Meditation?
- How many days did I do Mindful Memoirs?
- How many nights did I do Mindful Gratitudes?
- How many Mindful Exercises did I do?

TREE FROGS CHIRPING

LONELY TOO

IN THEIR OWN SPACE

W · E · E · K   F · O · U · R

Conscious Sexuality

The Third Mindfulness Training

Aware of the suffering caused by sexual misconduct, I am committed to cultivating responsibility and learning ways to protect the safety and integrity of individuals, couples, families, and society. I am determined not to engage in sexual relations without love and a long-term commitment. To preserve the happiness of others and myself, I am determined to respect my commitments and the commitments of others. I will do everything in my power to protect children from sexual abuse and to prevent couples and families from being broken by sexual misconduct.

Our society puts so much energy into stimulating sexual desire and "love" through various kinds of advertising, all of which seem to be totally unconnected to the commitment and true understanding that leads to real love. Sexual expression ought to be mutual, non–addictive, and not harmful to those involved.

The Third Mindfulness Training is all about the mind. If we keep this training in our minds and our hearts, we will be able to protect the happiness of others and ourselves. So many irresponsible

*Become the change
you want to see.*

–MAHATMA GANDHI

*It is not that mind-
fulness is the
'answer' to all
life's problems.
Rather, it is that
all life's problems
can be seen more
clearly through the
lens of a clear
mind.*

–JON KABAT-ZINN

sexual acts lead to tragedies in families. If we want a future to be possible for our children and the many generations that follow, we have to look at ourselves now for our actions today will affect the future.

In Eastern teachings, we speak of "oneness of body and mind." In the practice of modern psychology or Eastern medicine, simply looking at someone's face or body can tell us whether they suffer and are "dis–eased," or whether they are peaceful or healthy. What-ever happens in the body also happens in the mind. And likewise, when there is suffering in the mind, it shows in the body. When you are angry, you may think it is only in your feelings and your mind. But this is not true because when you are angry with some-one you love you don't want to touch or be touched by that per-son. So you see, body and mind are one.

In committed romantic relationships, there is communion of body and spirit. We open up our heart and soul to another. It is an act of creative energy. We do not open up our souls to just anyone, only to someone we love and trust. The same is true for our bod-ies. If we are approached casually, without care, we feel insulted both in our bodies and souls. If we are approached with under-standing, commitment, and care then we do not feel hurt, misused, or abused.

Love is attained through respect, commitment, and true under-standing. "Love" is a word used too casually by our Western soci-ety and by most advertising media. We have to look deeply at our speech. "Love" is a beautiful word worthy of the restoration of its true meaning. We can learn so much from this Third Mindfulness Training on conscious and responsible sex if we stop, concentrate, and gain insight.

Long-term Commitments

If we keep this training in our minds and our hearts we will be able to protect the happiness of others and ourselves. Sex can be a communion between two individuals and their spirits. True connection deserves respect and care. This Third Mindfulness Training is about deep caring and conscious, responsible sexuality.

If we understand love in its deepest way, and if love is real between two people, then why do we need a special wedding ceremony or a "long-term commitment"? Unconditional love has much responsibility attached to it; we are responsible to love that person for both their strengths and their weaknesses. All of us who have children know that we love them in spite of their warts, and that we give them so much of our understanding and patience. However, sometimes with our love-partners this type of unconditional love is a harder task! But the words "long-term commitment" help us understand the word "love." We cannot really love when we have only known a person for a few days. When we have children or a true friend, we do not turn around and say to them "I do not love you anymore." You need them, and they need you.

If you find someone with whom you want to share your life, then you face the challenge of sharing your whole life—your soul and your body. It's not an easy commitment and not one that everyone wants to make. If you chose this commitment, it is much easier with the support of family and friends. We all need this support, because our feelings for each other and our own practice are not always sufficient to sustain our happiness. There are many elements to any relationship, and one of them is supportive family and friends.

Being "in love" is very different—it is almost a sickness. And it is

Easy to do are things that are bad and harmful to oneself, but exceedingly difficult to do are things that are good and beneficial.

–UNKNOWN

the attachment to that other person that gives us this sickness. Some people can become addicted to this feeling of attachment; it almost becomes a drug to them. Although it makes us feel terrific, it isn't very peaceful. We become lovesick from being in love. We cannot think of anything but the object of our passion and we find it hard to work, study, and sometimes to sleep. It is a possessive and greedy love. We want that person to be totally ours, and we use that person to satisfy our own needs and desires.

In sexual relationships people can get hurt and wounded. Women often think it is only they who get wounded; however, men also get deeply hurt. So we have to be very careful in short-term relationships and use the Third Mindfulness Training to keep peace in others and ourselves. One of the problems is the feeling of loneliness in our world. Often we do not have real communication between ourselves and others, and we come to believe that having a sexual relationship will help us feel less lonely. This is very far from the truth. If there is no communication between two people, then a sexual relationship will widen this gap. They will both suffer, and will only feel more isolated afterwards.

The heart and the spirit have to be in union before the coming together of two bodies. Maybe the answer to loneliness is deep communication. Initial passion can be very strong and can absorb our whole being. However, we feel much calmer and more peaceful when, with deeper understanding and communication, the overcoming of day-to-day difficulties has been worked out over time. You might begin with passion, but as you live together and overcome difficulties, love and understanding deepen. This love has more wisdom and more unity. You feel gratitude for the other person, support, and great companionship. You feel understood by the other person and this creates happiness. This is the type of love that we need for families and society and it can only be obtained by long–term commitment.

REFLECTION:
A VERY SPECIAL WEDDING CEREMONY

The following is a letter that I wrote to my only brother Robin who lives in the U.K.

Dearest Robin,
You have asked me to write to you about the wedding. Thirty-five years ago you were unable to attend our wedding in England, and this year you were unable to attend our second son's wedding day in Canada. I know and understand why you were unable to celebrate these two days with me, although I am also sad about it.

But about Mark and Angela's wedding. Last October while on holiday in Barcelona, Mark dropped down to his knees and asked Angela to marry him and elope while they were in Spain. They talked about it, but in their hearts they knew it was important to be surrounded and supported by family and friends while making such a life-changing commitment. Being mindful, simple-living, and non-consumerist young folk, they decided to arrange their own very uncomplicated and beautiful wedding day.

The setting was a very warm day on a wonderfully peaceful raspberry farm just north of Toronto, with rolling green

It is simple to be happy, but oh so difficult to be simple.

–RINPOCHE IN SHIMLA

In the end the only things that really matter are how much did you love, how much did you live, and how well did you learn to let go.

—TAO TE CHING

Ontario countryside as a backdrop. Mark and some of his guests were already there. He was very relaxed and just putting the finishing touches to the marriage certificate table. They had invited only eighty people—half were family or family friends. They had arranged the whole day themselves and told us: if you start with a simple idea it is easy to keep things simple.

We sat in the chairs that had been set up near a very old oak tree. I saw a muscle move in my son's cheek and followed his gaze. He was watching Angela walk toward him, holding her mother and father's hands.

Angela was stunningly radiant. Their vows were beautiful and simple. From the moment Angela appeared, the sun shone for the rest of the evening until a nearly full moon came out later that night. The ceremony was simple and very emotional. Afterwards, Mark's brother Timothy and a friend, both great photographers, took some photos of their special day of commitment while water and other drinks were served to the guests.

Simple candle-lit tables awaited us in the tent for the buffet meal, a roasted pig on a spit (a Croatian tradition) with roasted vegetables and delicious salads for those of us who are vegetarians. Angela's parents are of Croatian and Italian heritage, and their Croatian friends had made a mountain of homemade traditional desserts.

Speeches were minimal with the two dads, the two maids of honor, and the best man saying just a few words, and Mark replying eloquently. A friend was asked to act as DJ and the dancing started with the bride and groom dancing to their favorite song. Angela then danced with her dad while I danced with Mark—what a very special happy proud moment for me! Then the fun really began with Angela's dad's old soccer team and their wives dancing the night away to Croatian music and songs. The evening flew by. The next day the wedding couple joined the whole family for an Indian meal and a walk by Lake Ontario. I am so proud to be their Mother.

In gratitude and with so much love,
Jeanie

How does all this relate to this training or to mindfulness? A commitment ceremony can be a ritual of excess or it can be a moment to celebrate mindful sexuality and mindful consumption. If you chose to have a ceremony to celebrate your commitment with another person, it can be an opportunity to practice the way you want your lives to be together and a way to give back to those people who have supported you and your relationship.

The purpose of life is to know oneself. We cannot do it unless we identify ourselves with all that lives.

–GANDHI

Sexual Abuse

In the Third Mindfulness Training it also states, "I will do everything in my power to protect children from sexual abuse.…" Adults who have been sexually abused as children suffer very much. Their whole life is affected daily by the abuse they suffered as children. To transform this suffering, they can use the Third Mindfulness

*...when we strive
to become better
than we are,
everything
around us
becomes
better, too.*

–PAULO COELHO

Training to help other children. Also, those who made us suffer can become the object of our love and protection. With love and understanding the men and women who have abused others can be helped. In many cases, they were the subject of sexual abuse themselves when they were children.

Sexual abuse relies on an imbalance of power between two individuals; in any sexual relationship an imbalance of power is unacceptable. So, as we vow to help and protect the children who have been abused, we can help the abusers who were children once themselves. They are all a product of our diseased society.

This training is also about freedom. As the power of mindfulness increases in ourselves, we become more aware of our thoughts, feelings, and actions. This allows us to make more informed and aware choices. And when we make a different or better choice, we have the chance to make a change. Mindfulness allows us to recognize that any of us could be a potential sexual abuser, and helps us accept the reality of this impulse and to let it go.

So you see, mindfulness gives us the freedom to make a different decision. This training is all about personal responsibility. We are all personally responsible for our own thoughts, actions, and feelings. However, when we live in a community, whether it is with only one other person or many, we are always responsible to others. This training can help us understand this difference and allow us to be responsible for not only our own behavior, but also the behavior of nations, corporations, and other institutions.

Following these trainings lets us become more powerful in terms of social change. That's because political change is actually an extension of our own personal values and lifestyle. Imagine a world where individuals and institutions treated each other with compassion, understanding, and loving kindness, where individuals truly protected the lives of each other and where the resources of this beautiful Earth were used for the enrichment of life rather than the destruction of it.

The Third Mindfulness Training is about all of this, for when we learn individually to cultivate responsibility and learn ways to protect the safety and integrity of individuals, couples, families, and society, we are doing the only thing an individual can do—changing ourselves. For as we all know, change can only begin with us. And when we change, everyone else begins to change.

Mindful Exercises

Start with small ideas. Remember, you cannot run a marathon before you learn to run around the block! The exercises below are to help you have greater understanding of yourself. When you understand your uniqueness, you can begin to love yourself and not hurt yourself with your own mind. Then you begin to understand and love others for their uniqueness.

- This week, notice how often sexual thoughts arise in your mind. Whenever they do, make a note of what feelings you find are associated with these thoughts. They may be feelings of love, caring, tension, compulsion, loneliness, greed, pleasure, or aggression. Try to name the feelings that you associate with different sexual thoughts.
- Get in touch with your creativity. Write a list of ten things you would like to create for yourself. Then write a list of ten things you would like to create for others.
- Cook a meal from a different region or country.
- Design and write a card to send to a friend.

- Make a small potted flower or herb garden.
- Write a poem about a simple daily happening.
- Write a list of your real needs from a relationship, leaving out anything sexual.
- Write about how you like people to physically touch you. Where on your body? For how long? How lightly or strongly? Stationary or moving? Tightly or loosely? Hugs or handshakes?

Mindful Memoirs: Age Fifteen to Age Twenty-one

By now you are beginning to know the routine. Take one or more Mindful Memoirs question each day and write for three or four pages. Use the list of ideas from below to get you started.

- Describe your life briefly as a teenager and young adult.
- How were these years fun for you? How were they difficult?
- What were some of the rules that you disliked at this time?
- If you had to tell the summary of your high school years, what would it be?
- What teachers, subjects, friends, and family members do you especially remember from this time?
- Write about one happening that you remember vividly during this period of your life. Look deeply into its significance.
- How well did your family teach you about the sex?
- How was your first date, if it was during this period? What did you do on dates? Write about the first person you fell in love with and his or her qualities and values.

- Describe your five closest friends during this time. Are there any patterns to your friendships? What influence did they have upon you?
- Write about your first real job during this time (even if it was only a part-time job).
- Write about your relationship with your parents, and how you were different and how you were the same as they.
- Write about the things you did to change your appearance during these years, and how your culture influenced this. How conscious were you of your physical appearance?
- What were your favorite sports or hobbies during this time? What books did you like to read? What was your favorite movie at this time?
- What type of music did you enjoy? Did you like dancing? Did you sing or learn to play an instrument?
- Write about a "turning point" in your life during those years.
- Write about how you felt when you first moved away from home, if it was during this period. How different was living on your own from your parents' home?
- The major accomplishment in my life during this period was…
- What did you want to be when you "grew up"?
- Who and what had the greatest influence on you during this period?
- When were you first aware of your sexuality and to whom were you attracted? How did this affect you?
- If you did go on to college, university, business school, or military service, write about how it affected you.
- Who do you still know from this period of your life?

- What dreams or goals did you set for yourself during these years? Write about how close you have come to realizing these dreams.

Weekly Check-in

Be kind, compassionate, accepting, and honest with yourself.

- How many days did I do Mindful Meditation?
- How many days did I do Mindful Memoirs?
- How many nights did I do Mindful Gratitudes?
- How many Mindful Exercises did I do?

NOW COMPLETE ACCEPTANCE

THE NEXT MOMENT, GONE

W · E · E · K F · I · V · E

Mindful Speech and Listening

The Fourth Mindfulness Training

Aware of the suffering caused by unmindful speech and the inability to listen to others, I am committed to cultivating loving speech and deep listening in order to bring joy and happiness to others and relieve others of their suffering. Knowing that words can create happiness or suffering, I am determined to learn to speak truthfully, with words that inspire self-confidence, joy, and hope. I will not spread news that I do not know to be certain and will not criticize or condemn things of which I am not sure. I will refrain from uttering words that can cause division or discord, or that can cause the family or the community to break. I am determined to make all efforts to reconcile and resolve all conflicts.

The Fourth Mindfulness Practice Training is for most people the hardest training to practice—our tongues have started more wars and created more suffering than any other muscle in our entire bodies!

A number of mindfulness students call this the "Oh dear" training. As in, "Oh dear, I forgot to use mindful speech." This is perhaps one of the hardest of the trainings, maybe because we all want to have our say! I have been a person to speak my mind without thinking too much. Mindfulness has helped me by stopping, breathing, and then speaking, but my family may not agree with that statement! I actually find that this practice is hardest with those with whom I am most intimate, my husband and children.

Often I find myself saying, "Oh dear, I wasn't really deeply listening to my partner, children, friend, boss or coworker." How often do we tune out the other person or how often does our mind go into thinking–mode as to what we are going to say next? To help with this, I have found that if I look into the other person's eyes directly then it really helps me to listen more deeply.

I also find that when someone is suffering emotionally, I am better able to stop and listen well. I empathize with their feelings and recognize the values behind their speech, rather than just hear their story. Where I have to be more mindful is when it is just day-to-day conversation. A technique I have found helpful is to remember, "To take each step in mindfulness" or "To speak/listen each word in mindfulness." Thich Nhat Hanh also encourages the practice of mindful speech and listening, using the Peace Treaty, and writing a Peace Note when anger or suffering arises between two or more people. The text of the Peace Treaty and the Peace Note is included in Appendix E. Thich Nhat Hanh writes:

> Learning to speak with loving kindness is crucial to restoring peace and harmony in our relationships and our environment. You need to tell the other person about your suffering and pain, especially with the people you love the most. But we only use loving speech.

We say the truth in a loving and nonviolent way. Only when we use loving speech will the other person be able to listen.

Speech can be constructive or destructive. So when we feel irritated, we should refrain from saying anything. We can just breathe, or we can practice walking meditation in the fresh air, looking at the sky, the grass, the trees. Once our calm and serenity are restored, we are able again to use the language of loving kindness. While we are speaking, if we feel our irritation coming up again, we can stop and breathe. The basis of loving speech is our practice of mindfulness. Mindfulness helps us restore communication, first within ourselves, and then with others. Our mindful speech nourishes our own mindfulness and produces mindfulness in the other person. With our daily practice of mindfulness, we cultivate the capacity to speak lovingly and also the capacity to listen deeply to the suffering of the other person. There is a practice that can help bring peace into your family and your relationships, and that is the practice of the Peace Treaty. We sign a peace treaty with each other, and this gives us a way to practice when we are too angry or upset to express ourselves calmly. The Peace Treaty offers practices for the person on each side of the situation. If we are upset, we need to express this to the other person within twenty-four hours. If we are not calm enough to speak, we may find it useful to send them a peace note.

Mindful Listening

Deep listening is a skill that takes many years to develop. It requires concentrating completely in order to understand what that other person is really saying. This means not just listening to the words, but also to the feelings behind the words. When we do this, we can begin to understand the other person a little better.

In his book *Calming the Fearful Mind*, Thich Nhat Hanh answers a question posed to him by an interviewer soon after September 11, 2001: "What would you say to Osama bin Laden if you had the chance to meet him?" Nhat Hanh responded that if given the opportunity to come face to face with Osama bin Laden, the first thing he would do would be to listen. He would try to understand why bin Laden had acted in the ways he has. He would try to understand all of the suffering that had led him to such violence. He said it might not be easy to listen in that way, so he would remain calm and lucid. He would need several friends with him who are also strong in the practice of deep listening, to listen without reacting, without judging or blaming.

It is a sad reflection of our busy society that many of us have to spend money on counselors or therapists just to get someone to really listen to us. Thich Nhat Hanh's response to this question reminded me once again to bring this precious and skillful practice into my everyday life, to try to just listen deeply. Try it today with someone you love. I am sure the result can only bring you both greater acceptance and understanding.

What Kind of a Listener Are You?

Why do we not listen to others? Often we hear what is said, but more often we don't listen to what is really being said. Hearing the feelings behind the words is an art—the art of listening mindfully.

I read somewhere that there are many kinds of listeners. There are Mind Readers—those folk who usually hear nothing while they are thinking in their minds, "What is this person really feeling or thinking?" Then there are the listeners who are called Rehearsers. They are so busy thinking about what they want to say, they never hear a word you are saying.

Ever met a Filterer? These are often people who are very close to us, partners, parents, or sometimes our own children. A Filterer is a selective listener, hearing only what they want to hear! I used to sometimes say that my four children were "mother-deaf"!

Do you know an Identifier? These folk always identify everything you say with one of their own experiences (and usually it's a bigger and a better story than your own). Then there are the Comparers—people who get sidetracked assessing or judging you, rather than listening to your message. I know lots of these people!

I'm sure you've all met (or, like me, at times have been) the Derailer. The Derailer always changes the subject quickly, to let you know that they are not interested in anything you have to say. A Sparrer is almost the same as a Derailer; they hear what is said, but quickly belittle or discount it. Then there is the Placater. They agree with everything you say, just to be nice or to avoid confrontation, which means they really don't hear a thing you say.

So what type of listener are you? I certainly know that I fall into each of the categories some of the time! And sometimes, when I have been able to breathe and be present, I can be a Mindful Lis-

Where you tend a rose, my lad, a thistle cannot grow.

—THE SECRET GARDEN

tener. I haven't mastered this difficult skill yet, however, I do have a couple of techniques that I have found helpful.

First, start by looking directly at the other person. This focuses your mind and keeps it from wandering off. Second, come back to your breath. During the time I am listening, I follow my breathing. If I become distracted, one conscious breath is enough to bring my mind back to my body and I can listen more intently to what is being said. Deep listening is an art that takes some practice, especially if we want to be able to listen to the harsh language, judgments, recriminations, and misperceptions that might be voiced by a loved one who feels hurt. It is important to listen without reacting so they can have the relief that comes from saying what is in their heart. There is always time later on to correct their misperceptions little by little. But at the time we are listening to them, it is important that we not say anything. That is why it is important to follow our breathing and remember why we are listening—to give them relief and let them feel they have really been heard. If we interrupt or answer back, we will destroy this precious opportunity. If we feel we cannot take anymore, then we can say, "Darling, I'm a little bit tired. Could we continue tomorrow?" As we continue making mindful meditation and the exercises in this book a part of our daily life, our ability to listen will increase.

In his teachings on the Seven Spiritual Laws of Success, Deepak Chopra expands on a teaching of the Buddha, saying:

> This existence of ours is as transient as autumn clouds.
> To watch the births and deaths of beings is like looking
> at the movement of a dance; a lifetime is like a flash of
> lightning in the sky, flashing by like a torrent down the
> steep mountain. We have stopped for a moment to

encounter each other, to meet, to love, to share. This is a precious moment, but it is transient. It is a little parenthesis in eternity. If we share with caring, light heartedness, and love, we will create abundance and joy for each other and then this moment will have been worthwhile.

REFLECTION: LADY DIANA

I have a brand new older friend. I call her Lady Diana, and she is a very compassionate listener. Diana Williams is in her eighties and is well known in Bermuda for her beautiful doll making skills. Diana is full of life and a delight to be with. As a young person, Diana had always wanted to be a fashion designer, and even submitted her drawings as a teenager to an art college. However, World War II came along and, at the tender age of sixteen, she trained to be a nurse. In fact at that time she was the youngest person ever to graduate from the five-year nurse's training at Guy's Hospital in London, England.

In 1952, she married an English golf professional. For their honeymoon they traveled, or as she said, "motored," all across the United States. They ended up on Long Island, where they lived happily for nine years. Afterwards, she and her husband moved to Bermuda, where he worked as the pro at a golf club. But when a terrible bike accident ended his career, Diana had to use her old nursing skills to support the family.

All you need to do to receive guidance is to ask for it and then listen.

–SANAYA ROMAN

About ten years ago Lady Diana saw in Bermuda an exhibition of dolls by Kath Bell. Kath taught her how to make her first Christmas Doll. It was through Kath and her patience that Lady Diana developed her artistic expertise. She has been eternally thankful and joyful for the gift of her mentorship. The expressions of her creative talents that started with Kath's teaching have given her lasting pleasure in her senior years. Diana was so clever and skillful and so adored designing and dressing the dolls, that one year she made ten antique dolls for a local jeweler's windows. A week later she proudly took her children into Hamilton to see her beautiful work. But sadly, the dolls were no longer there, as a collector had fallen in love with them and bought them all!

Once, while at a senior's art class at the Bermuda College, Lady Diana showed me an example of mindful listening. A handsome young student called Jeremy wheeled into our class in his wheelchair. Diana asked him how and when his accident had occurred, and how he felt about it. He brushed her off at first, but she encouraged him with her deep listening skills and mindful speech. She was totally present for him, in her body language, her words, and her feedback. She truly heard what he was saying and also heard the feelings behind the words. It was a total joy for them both, a joy for all of us present, and a lesson in mindful speech and listening. Diana's skills reminded me once again to bring this precious skill, at all times, into my everyday life.

Compassionate "Deep Values" Listening

I once read an article about compassionate listening in which the author wrote about realizing that the anger that had plagued her all her life came from times when she didn't feel acknowledged or understood. In other words, all her anger stemmed simply from not being heard. She also talked about how powerful storytelling is to any healing process. She described a powerful storytelling technique that can be used by groups of four people. One person tells their story, while the other three listen. One listens to the story line, one listens to the emotions and feelings being expressed, while the last listens to the underlying values. When the speaker finishes, the other three give feedback about what they heard. When the person hears the feedback about the values that they had expressed, it is a great comfort and relief. You see, when we understand where the other person is truly coming from, we can find commonalities and begin to heal the vast differences that can overwhelm us in our communication and our lives.

A Quaker peace activist who pioneered compassionate listening and has been involved in some of the world's greatest conflicts over the past thirty years suggests that we examine ourselves and discover what it is we find hard to listen to. Then we have to discipline ourselves not to react. We have to discern the real truth—and that is not heard with the human ear, it is heard by listening with our spiritual ears or our heart ears. She has found that compassionate listening has made for some transforming experiences, usually both for the listener and the speaker. Learning about each other as human beings and potential friends means we also gain new understandings about others and ourselves. It is very much a

Listening is a form of accepting.

–STELLA TERRILL MANN

reciprocal experience to listen compassionately to another without interrupting.

REFECTION: JIM'S FUNERAL

James Smith—better known as Jim—died in March of 2003.

Jim and Ann Smith were some of kindest people my husband and I met when we first moved to Bermuda. Just before we moved here, we came down for a short visit to find somewhere to live. We stayed at Ann's beautiful guesthouse in Hamilton. She immediately took us under her wing and helped us in all sorts of ways, so much so that we nicknamed her "The Bermuda Oracle."

While we were staying at her guesthouse, she invited us out to her magnificent home to meet Jim and to have afternoon tea. My husband and I were both very flattered and had a wonderful afternoon with them. From this very first kind and most generous act, we formed a closeness. So it was with immense sadness that we heard from Ann the news of Jim's death.

At Jim's funeral, the minister acknowledged Jim's life. He used careful words of great comfort. One of Jim's closest friends told the complete story of Jim's life and all about the man he knew and loved as one of his best friends. This is something we expect to happen at funerals, a mindfully spoken tribute or eulogy about the person who has just died.

I remember when my husband John celebrated a "big" birthday, I wanted to pay tribute to him right then, rather than waiting for someone else to do so after his passing. So I spent many hours writing and editing a personal tribute to read to him, with only our immediate family present, on his special day. It was actually quite a tough thing to write and to read, because the better we know someone, the harder it is for us to describe how we actually feel about him or her! I told the story of what he had done and "been" in his life; however, I wanted to go much deeper and tell him what he truly meant to his family, his friends, and to me.

We all have such little time on this Earth to do and say the things that are important to us and make that moment worthwhile. It was only later that I realized that all the qualities I had described in my tribute to John, I had also recognized in our dear friend Jim. I am not sure, but maybe this is what Ann also saw in Jim, and perhaps in John too, and maybe this is one of the reasons she extended such loving kindness to us when we first came into her life. They say that people come into our lives for a lifetime, a season, or a reason. Jim came into Ann's life for a lifetime. That I know. Ann and Jim came into our lives for both a season and a reason. That I know. And I know it was to teach us about mindful listening and speech, generosity, and true loving kindness.

*Change the
story and you
will change
the perception,
change the
perception
and you change.*

–UNKNOWN

Mindful Exercises

Just as the North Star or the sun can be used as a guide to get us somewhere, we also know that they are both impossible to reach. Hopefully by now you are getting some idea of the help offered by the Five Mindfulness Trainings. Your effort is only to proceed in their direction; there is no destination to reach, only a journey. The scope of these trainings will influence your conduct, habits, character, and mental states. By practicing only one of the five Mindfulness Trainings, you will become more aware, calm, concentrated, and closer to an enlightened life.

Right now in this fifth week you may be feeling unmotivated. The three practices of Mindful Meditation, Mindful Memoirs, and Mindful Gratitudes may seem about as enticing as a bowl of cold lumpy porridge on a damp foggy morning. However, congratulate yourself on getting this far and remember that this is about making major changes. It will continue to take a lot of discipline, determination, and commitment. There might be times when you're tired, sad, stressed, angry, and confused—times when all that will matter to you will be making yourself feel better straightaway. But it will be during these times that you'll really need to focus on why you started in the first place! Also ask your Mindful Way Group—which, hopefully you have formed—for help. After all, that is why they are there to assist you.

Of course, the occasional slip–up isn't the end of the world, but if those slip–ups become regular, you may be tempted to give up. It might not be easy, but it will be worth it to finish the next three weeks. There is a lot to be said about individual learning, self-awareness, self-reflection, and solitude time. Be it the meditation, the memoirs journaling, or the nightly gratitudes, there is learning that is happening when we give ourselves the time to be with our experience, reflect, explore, and absorb the lessons. Taoism talks about understanding the universe through individual practices, and there are other Eastern philosophies that take the same perspective. However, I can also see the other side of the argument as well. Many of my learning experiences have occurred in workshops, groups, or conversations with others. I often see myself through an experience of someone else in a particular group and get my own learning this way. And it often doesn't matter whether I am a participant or wearing the facilitator's hat—the learning is there if and when I choose to be open to it.

Change can happen in an instant if you are determined to change. It is deciding to make the change that can take a lot longer. If you want to change something, stop holding on to it. Start new habits. Start where you are today. Yesterday and the past are like last month's Sunday dinners—long gone. Today gives you a fresh start and the way your mind thinks right now will shape your tomorrow. What is important is taking responsibility for yourself and always being alert to your mind. It is we who are the creators of joy and magic, of sorrow, or of peace in our lives. I truly believe that following these practices is a way of allowing our life to flow, rather than letting events get in the way and causing us much grief and unhappiness. Remember, any change of habit takes a minimum of thirty days to transform. You are now at that stage, five weeks into the course. Congratulations to you!

- Practice breathing three times before you speak and see if what you have to say is really necessary. Write about the experience.
- Ask yourself before you speak, "Is what I am going to say kind, is it true, and is it necessary?"

Equanimity is a profound quality of mindfulness that cultivates the ability to let go.

–TARA BENNETT-GOLDMAN

- Practice smiling before you speak. Thich Nhat Hanh suggests: "Step back, let go, and return to the island of self." Allow yourself to smile and breathe, feel the feelings in the space and understanding will arise. This is a hard practice but a miracle worker.

- When someone or something upsets you this week, ask yourself, "Do I suffer because of my lack of understanding?" Write about the insights you gain from this practice.

- The expression, "When in Rome, do as the Romans do" is so true. Use this practice when you are dealing with someone from a culture different from your own. In other words, wherever you go in life, just like when you go on vacation, don't pack too much baggage, only pack an open (and mindful) mind. See how this practice works for you this week.

- Create a breathing area/room in your home. This is a space or place where you can go if you are angry, distressed, or upset. Make it a special space with a warm blanket on the floor and some flowers and candles. If you are feeling upset or angry, go there and breathe for at least fifteen minutes or practice walking meditation in this room or space.

- Write about what you are "tolerating in your life" at the moment. Write out the first five steps to making a change. This is a very powerful exercise.

- Don Miguel Ruiz of the Toltec tradition tells us about the Four Agreements: "I am impeccable with my word. I don't take anything personally. I never make assumptions. I always do my best." Try exercising any one of these four principles daily during this week.

- Every day this week, tell at least three people how you appreciate them; use their names and say thank you.
- Try using "the sandwich" method when you have to critique someone or tell him or her how you are feeling about a negative situation. Begin with the positive, then add the constructive and critical, then finish with something positive. This is like a sandwich, with the critique being the filling between two positive pieces of bread. Always praise or compliment the person first, then using "I statements" so you are only expressing your own feelings, tell them how you are feeling, then finish with another positive comment. An example would be, "Your bright enthusiasm is one of the highlights of my day. Today I felt I couldn't be heard because you seemed distracted. I'm sorry if something is getting in the way of your usual shining energy today."
- Allow the phone to ring three times, taking two or three breaths before answering it. Then you will really "be there" both for yourself and the other person when you pick up the receiver.

Mindful Memoirs: Age Twenty-two to Twenty-eight

Note: If you are not yet twenty–eight, just write up to whatever age you are!

- Write about the most significant event(s) that happened to you during this period.
- Make a list of jobs you had during this time. Write about

Gratitude is not only the greatest of virtues, but the parent of all others.

–CICERO, 54 BC

the best job or supervisor you had during this period and/or the worst job or boss you had. Did you like your work during this time? Where were you "at" during this time of your working life?

■ What accomplishments in your education or career were you proud of at this time? What would you prefer to forget? Would you have chosen the same path if you had the chance to do it all again?

■ Write about how different or similar you were from your parents at this time of your lives. Look also at the historical/social/economic conditions of your life and your parents'.

■ Were you in a long-term relationship during this period? Write about how you felt about it then and how you feel now. Describe what attracted you to your partner. In what ways were you alike? In what ways were you different?

■ If you were single during this time frame, describe what your life was like. Did you find making decisions alone difficult or liberating? Were there periods of loneliness? Was it your choice to be single?

■ Write about any births and deaths you experienced during this period.

■ What were your career/education dreams during this time period? Did you fulfill them?

■ Write about where you lived during these seven years and how you felt about your home(s).

■ How much contact did you have with your family during this period? How did you get along with your parents and/or siblings at this time?

■ Write about what has really changed in you from childhood to this time in your adulthood.

- Who was your best friend at this time of your life? Write about the values and gifts he/she possessed and why you like him/her.
- Write about your greatest strengths and values at this time of your life.
- Write about how you spent your free time during this period.
- How well did you communicate with others during this period of your life? Were you actually who you were, in what you said and how you acted? Be honest with yourself.
- What risks did you take during this period?
- Did you consider yourself to be traditional, modern, or unconventional during this time?

Weekly Check-in

Be kind, compassionate, accepting, and honest with yourself.

- How many days did I do Mindful Meditation?
- How many days did I do Mindful Memoirs?
- How many nights did I do Mindful Gratitudes?
- How many Mindful Exercises did I do?

WAVES REFLECT

THE MOON

ON THE STONE HARBOR WALLS

W · E · E · K   S · I · X

Mindful Consumption

The Fifth Mindfulness Training

Aware of the suffering caused by unmindful consumption, I am committed to cultivating good health, both physical and mental, for myself, my family, and my society by practicing mindful eating, drinking, and consuming. I will ingest only items that preserve peace, well-being, and joy in my body, in my consciousness, and in the collective consciousness of my family and society. I am determined not to use alcohol or any other intoxicant, or to ingest foods or other items that contain toxins, such as certain TV programs, magazines, books, films, and conversations. I am aware that to damage my body or my consciousness with these poisons is to betray my ancestors, my parents, my society, and future generations. I will work to transform violence, fear, anger, and confusion in myself and in society by practicing a diet for myself and for society. I understand that a proper diet is crucial for self-transformation and for the transformation of society.

REFLECTION: SANDPIPERS ON THE BEACH

The 9/11 terrorist attacks in the U.S. have made many of us think deeply upon our own future and the future of our precious planet. In a letter written after the attacks, Thich Nhat Hanh reflected on cultivating compassion in response to violence as a way to peace. He reminds us, "We are all co-responsible for the making of violence and despair in the world by our way of living, consuming, and of handling the problems of our world."

I have thought deeply about this statement. I have tried to "walk in the shoes" of the perpetrators of these terrible acts of violence. I have tried to imagine what in their own lives may have happened and what those of us in the U.S. and Western European nations may have done to create such hatred and violence. Who had hurt them so terribly that they had to strike back at those unknown victims? I did this in order to try to understand them more deeply. It has been said that we are all interconnected on this Earth by only six degrees of separation, so how has my way of living and consuming made me co-responsible for this violence?

The Western world consumes most of the world's resources, while the rest of the world is left with very little. Where is the equality in these statistics? Mindless consumption is part of this problem. I have been part of this problem, having lived through and been caught up in the "me generation" of the "got to have it all" period of the 1980s. Having worked as a volunteer in palliative care, I now know that at the end of most people's lives, the only thing of any real importance is their relationships with family and friends—definitely not their possessions!

The day after Hurricane Erin left Bermuda's beaches somewhat changed, I was walking in the early morning along the South Shore and noticed that the sandpiper birds had found hundreds of tiny dead silver fish that had been marooned on the beach by the high tides. Then I saw something strange. The birds had so much food to choose from, they were just pecking small holes into each fish's side, and then abandoning them. It made me reflect on how we in the West often shop until we drop, just to use or wear a product once and then never look at it or use it again. Is this mindful consumption? Are we adding to the despair and violence in the world by our way of consuming and living?

Over the last decades, the Western world has been involved daily in major wars, and has killed tens of thousands of innocent people and produced more weapons, including weapons of mass destruction. In the meantime, 40,000 children die every day of preventable diseases and millions do not have enough food, drinkable water, electricity, housing, health care, or education. Any hope for our future world depends on the West becoming peaceful with all nations by consuming less, showing compassion, understanding, acceptance, and kindness, rather than. As Martin Luther King, Jr. said, being the "greatest purveyors of violence in the world."

Mental formations are in every cell of the body.

–THICH NHAT HANH

Mindful Consumption and Mindful Eating

The more mindfully we live, the more mindfully we will eat. We could all live much more mindfully when it comes to day-to-day consumption. In many parts of Europe, Central and South America, and Africa, marketing is done daily in open-air markets. Food is wrapped in paper rather than plastic, or is not wrapped at all.

When I take a shower, I look at my body that was given as a gift from my parents and I ask myself, to whom does my body really belong? Who gave me this body? In my meditation I see that all my ancestors and all the future generations are present in my body. When I see this, I know what I have to do and what I "should" not do. I see that I really do not have a separate self. I am not living as a separate entity. I am my parents, I am past generations, and future generations. So whatever I ingest physically or mentally, I do it for everyone. This is one way this Fifth Mindfulness Training can be practiced.

If you do not have a good relationship with your parents or children, it might be because there are parts of yourself that you do not love. To love yourself is to love your parents and your children. In today's world of individualism, people think they have the right to live their own lives, without answering to anyone. However, the reality is that we do not have a separate self. We are a part of past and future generations and all other living beings. We are connected to clouds, rain, and earth, because we have ingested these in the food that nourishes us. The water we drink and the air we breathe are also part of us and part of the whole cosmos. So by keeping our bodies healthy, we are really creating the health of and expressing gratefulness to the whole universe. This is the concept of interbeing. We can get out of our small "self" shell and see that we are interrelated to everyone and everything in this world. Our every act is linked with the whole of person–kind.

Mindful consumption is the object of the Fifth Training, because we are what we eat. We have to drink and eat. However, we can do it mindfully. We can be in touch with our food. We can show gratitude for our food. We can start by eating at least one meal a day mindfully. Before eating we can give thanks in the form of a grace for our food, and as we eat we can call our food by its true name. Naming a food helps us to get in touch with our food on a more direct level. For example, by naming a potato, we can look deeper into the nature of the potato, look at how it began as a seed potato, and contemplate the soil it was grown in, the rain that fell on it, the farmer, the trucker, and the shopkeeper who are all part of that potato. Ultimately, this is a meditation on how we are a part of everything and everybody in this universe.

Mindful eating is a practice of living in consciousness. I have found that children also enjoy doing this (as long as you show them how), particularly when it comes to naming the item to be eaten and looking at all that is in it or has in some way touched it during the course of its journey to our tables. Mindful eating can transform your life from disease to health. Why would I choose to have disease in my life when I can have a healthy life? Mindfulness is all about finding peace within us. Isn't that what many of us wish for—peace on Earth? But remember, in reality, it all begins with individuals—you and me.

Desire is like the thin cow's skin, it absorbs everything.

–THICH NHAT HANH

*True life is lived
when tiny
changes occur.*

–LEO TOLSTOY

REFLECTION: FARMERS' MARKET

For some time now I have been getting up early every weekend to support my local farmers' market. A visit to any farmers' market gives you a chance to meet some of the nicest people and buy some of the freshest produce. It is also one of the most mindful ways of producing and consuming.

A woman named Frances started the Bermuda Farmer's Market. She got the idea while sitting on the Board of Agriculture where she continually heard about and recognized the challenges that Bermuda's farmers face and the threats to Bermuda's arable land. She had extra produce from her own garden, and she realized she could either give it away, sell it from a small roadside stand, or simply let it rot.

So with a lot of courage and the help of her son, Frances got a group of people together to support her idea of a local farmers' market. She is there every Saturday morning selling her own extra produce and big bags of horse manure. She also provides coffee and homemade muffins for the shoppers.

There are now many people who sell their goods at the market. Katrina's passion and hobby is candy making. Her family kept suggesting that she send her candies to different stores, but she wanted to keep her honey, tea, lemon, and chocolate candies under her own control. So she changed her hobby into a little business. Then there's Sally and her jams and chutneys. She has been making them for ten years, and her customers, she is proud to tell you, are mostly locals. Her garden produces more bananas than she knows what to do with, so she also sells these along with her jams.

My favorite indulgence at the market is Margaret's dough-nuts. Well, actually they are Portuguese *malassadas*, originally only made for Ash Wednesday to finish up the animal lard before Lent. Now Margaret gets up at 2 am every Saturday morning with her biggest supporter and helper, her husband Gil, to make a couple hundred of these sugary delights (she now uses vegetable oil instead of the animal-based lard). Margaret and Gil are empty nesters and like to be busy, and they often make their doughnuts for school bazaars and church fairs as fundraisers. Her doughnuts are the most delicious treat of the week!

Then there is the honey man, Randolph—thirty-two years a beekeeper and the owner of Chartwell Apiaries, with his Bermuda honey and many "bee-attitudes." Always smiling behind his table and putting "I love you honey" stickers on all those who pass, he says that honey is the finest food on Earth and the only thing that never goes bad in your pantry. In 1986 he was the feature of the Agricultural Fair, the man with the Bee Beard. He told me that it was to demonstrate to people that bees will only sting if threatened—an interesting statement when we relate it to human relationships! He says he loves to be part of the market, because he gets to meet the nicest peo-ple. He told me that people are people and we all need each other. He recognizes the interbeing of all living things, animals, and of course, busy bees!

"Drink Your Health" juicing man Wayne makes fresh juices that contain carrot and rosemary for headaches, parsley and carrot for asthma, and many other combinations of fruits and vegetables that are perfect for curing other conditions. He got into juicing while conditioning his own body when he started long distance running.

Why not enjoy a mindful weekend morning and go and support your own local market, if one exists in your community? There you will meet lots of conscious folks, learn about your community, and become a fully aware and mindful consumer to boot!

Is Your Life Filled with Too Much Stuff?

Dr. David Suzuki, Canada's leading pioneer in ecological living, has said, "Most of us are quite aware of the harsh damage we are inflicting upon this precious Earth with our garbage. But sometimes we all feel so insignificant as individuals among our 6.2 billion people when it comes to making a change on this impact. It is damage we inflict upon this Earth with our excessive consumerism. And we all at times ask, what can we do?"

Everything is connected—no one thing can change by itself.

–PAUL HAWKEN

Only a half a century ago, prudence was considered a virtue. But now, with two thirds of the Earth's population having their economies based on consumerism, garbage has become a real problem. When I first visited Bermuda twenty-five years ago, I cannot remember any garbage strewn around. I unhappily cannot say the same today. From the time of the stock-market crash of 1929, the Great Depression, and the Second World War, consumerism has been the driving force behind the Western world's economies. Consumerism has become a way of life. Goods have become rituals—we no longer "want" stuff, we "need" stuff. And this stuff is consumed, burned up, replaced, and discarded faster and faster with every passing decade.

Consumerism has overtaken more important things in life. We have not concentrated on health care, education, sustainable housing or transportation, or providing for our own local underfed and under-cared for children. Instead, we've focused all our energies on providing the world with more consumer "stuff." Very often things are produced and then quickly thrown away (paper towels, tinfoil, plastic bottles, styrofoam food containers, coffee cups). Many products are made cheaply, so that the consumer market will never be saturated and more "stuff" can be produced. All of these products come from our Earth and are returned to the Earth as toxic matter.

The purchase of a lot of this "stuff" produces a natural high by boosting the self-esteem of the purchaser for a few hours, days, or maybe even months. But eventually, this effect wears off, and a sense of emptiness returns. Purchasing and collecting has reached such heights that people have had to build bigger houses and extra storage space in order to store their "stuff." We even have people running profitable businesses telling others how to organize and reduce their clutter. The idea of more gives some of us an added sense of security. So much of what we purchase is not essential for our basic comfort, but is based only on impulse desire. How often do you ask yourself, "Do my purchasing choices have social, spiritual, or ecological consequences?"

"Stuff" becomes clutter, and when we clutter up our lives, we find we don't have room for more important things. I have always said that we are born with nothing and that we leave with nothing. I try hard to practice following "a diet of mindful consumption as a way of self-transformation and for the transformation of

No trumpets sound when the important decisions of our life are made. Destiny is made known silently.

–AGNES DEMILLE

my society." I still have a number of mindless consumer weaknesses; however, I am aware that the things I consume and purchase can have much wider consequences.

REFLECTION: ON ORANGES

It was raining when I was traveling across Florida, the Sunshine State, by car. I knew that Florida was one of the world's largest producers of oranges and orange products; however, I had not realized that the state of Florida is also one the largest producers of beef in the U.S. This was confirmed as I passed by thousands of grazing cattle and millions of oranges. As with any long car journey, I used the time to meditate, but this time upon oranges!

In *Peace Is Every Step*, Thich Nhat Hanh suggests that every time you eat an orange, you do orange meditation. He asks, "When was the last time that you sat down and really enjoyed eating an orange, nothing else, just eating an orange, not talking to a friend while eating it, or watching the TV, or reading a newspaper while eating it? To live a fully mindful life we cannot do two things at once." Here is Thich Nhat Hanh's full orange meditation:

> We put the orange on the palm of our hand and look at it, breathing in a way that the orange becomes real. Most of the time when we eat a orange, we hardly look at it; we are thinking about many other things.

If we eat the orange in forgetfulness, the orange is not really there. But if we bring our mind and body back together and produce our true presence, becoming fully alive, then we see the orange is a miracle. The orange is an ambassador of the cosmos, a wonderful presence of life. So many causes and conditions have come together to make the orange possible—the sunshine, the rain, the soil, the farmer, the atmosphere. We see the blossom becoming the fruit, we can smell the blossom and the warm, moist earth. We really see the orange. As the orange becomes real, we become real, and life in that moment becomes real.

Mindfully we begin to peel the orange and notice the pungent fragrance of the skin as it breaks. We look at each section of the orange before we eat it. When we put it into our mouth and bite it, we feel the juice on our tongue. We are in touch with the orange, and we know it is really an orange. We are completely there with our orange, not in a rush, not thinking about anything else. We eat each section in perfect mindfulness until we have finished the entire fruit. Both the orange and the one who eats it become real. Doing activities in this way is the basic work for creating peace—in ourselves, in our relationships, and in the world.

In my orange meditation across Florida I wasn't actually eating an orange, but I meditated on the hundreds of oranges I

Perception is a mirror, not a fact. And what I look on is my state of mind reflected outwards.

–UNKNOWN

could see from out of the car window. I could see that each orange was full of the earth, the sky, and much loving hard work. Finally, after many hours of driving, I pulled over and rummaged in my bag. I pulled out a single orange, peeled it, and ate it. I could see that, with each bite of orange, I was part of the earth and the sky. I was also part of the hard work that has gone into cultivating those orange trees, from tiny saplings to fully-grown dark green beauties. As I chewed, I recognized my connection to the machines and the people who harvest the fully ripened fruits, to the people and trucks that take them to the juicing factories and markets for sale. I was also a part of the women and men who process them in the factories, and a part of the machines that juice the oranges. I was part of the plane that brings them to my home in Bermuda and the pilots that flew them here. Without these people I would never have this single orange. In one orange, there are so many layers of interconnection.

REFLECTION:
A COLORFUL HIBISCUS FLOWER

If there is anyone I have met who exemplifies "a mindful way" or living consciously, living in awareness, or living in the Now, it would be my dear friend Jim Humphreys. At

86, he really lives for each moment. He savors each moment that is given to him. Some would say that at such a great age it is the natural way of living, and maybe that is true. However, Jim joyfully tastes each moment that is given to him and never seems to put off until tomorrow what could be done today.

He tells me all the time he is "in training for life." He knows that he is still a student in the School of Life and loves every mindful moment of it. He reminds me of the beautiful hibiscus flowers in Bermuda that only last twenty-four hours. Every morning he blossoms anew, then at night, when he is so tired from living the day fully in awareness, he closes his petals and falls into a deep sleep. It is all a part of his "training program."

Jim first came to Bermuda as a young naval officer at the end of World War II, where he met his Bermudian wife-to-be Shirley. He says that she fell in love with him, but especially with his jeep. He was living fully in the moment even then— he married her just nine months later. The two of them went on to spend most of their married life in Detroit, where he worked for the Ford Motor Company. However, most of their vacations were spent in his wife's beloved Bermuda. When he retired twenty years ago, there was no decision to be made as to where they would live; Bermuda would again be their home. One of Jim's proudest memories is the volunteer work that Shirley did for the Bermuda Breast Cancer Group after she was diagnosed with the disease. She worked tirelessly for many years for this group.

When Shirley died, he volunteered to read the lesson at his church the very next Sunday. He was determined to live in the moment and live it fully in awareness or mindfulness. When he talks about Jay, his oldest son who died of a brain tumor at the age of fifty, a deep sadness glazes over his eyes. He acknowledges his loss and sadness and at once comes back to what is actually happening in the moment.

Although living very much in the moment, he is always planning his next step with his children, grandchildren, or with friends and neighbors. He loves to invite his young grandchildren to stay with him for vacations and arranges fun educational outings for them. He regularly attends mentally stimulating talks given on the island or takes his family or friends to his club for a meal. He attends church weekly. He has spent hours organizing his house and affairs, in the process of simplifying his life. Always aware of others, he says he wants to make things easy for his children, so that when he is finally "tucked in beside Shirley at St. Paul's Churchyard," he will have left nothing undone!

Jim's life of being "in training" is simple. He gets up each day and knows that he is going to enjoy it fully. He swims and walks daily, and mindfully watches his diet. He fully enjoys his family and friends. He is overjoyed to have a fax machine to keep in touch with his family in the U.S. He is so grateful every day for what he has, rather than what he doesn't have. He is a beautiful hibiscus flower in my life.

REFLECTION: FORTY DAYS OF CHANGE

My friend Carol came over for dinner and told me that she had given up drinking wine for Lent. She said that it was her practice every year to give up something during the weeks before Easter. Her remark reminded me of my dear friend Diane, who used to join me every week for a walk around magnificent Stanley Park in Vancouver, B.C., Canada.

One day while walking, Diane announced, "Jeanie, I am giving up coffee for Lent." I replied, "Oh, I didn't know that you were so religious." "I'm not," she responded.

Carol denied herself wine, while Diane denied herself coffee. Both enjoyed drinking these beverages; however, both felt they would benefit in some way from denying themselves. But their reasons for doing so were very different. Carol told me that each year she chooses one food or drink item to give up, usually beginning with the letter "C": cakes, candies, caramels, coffee, crisps, cookies, chocolate, Coke. This year was the same: chardonnay (along with other wines that didn't begin with a "C"). She told me that one of her reasons was that it cut back on calories (another "C"), and usually after the forty days she didn't have any interest in going back to eating or drinking the item she had given up. Also, an additional benefit is that she loses some curves and stops a craving (two other "C"s) for certain cooked items. She also feels more in control and enjoys the feeling of discipline.

The year my friend Diane gave up coffee for Lent, she had been going to Starbucks four to five times a day: before she drove to work; when she arrived at work; at midmorning coffee break; at teatime in the afternoon; and very often before she drove home. She often talked about not being able to afford to go away for a fun vacation, or to visit her mum in the United Kingdom. Together, we worked out the dollar cost of her six-day workweek coffee-drinking habit. She realized if she'd put her coffee money into a savings account, in a year she'd have about $4,000—enough to go away on a holiday.

Changing a habit for forty days is strong practice, and it often means that the change will become permanent. By doing this, both of my friends gained something. One developed a more mindful way of consuming (along with the loss of a few pounds and the gain of a much healthier body), while the other gained more cash in her savings account and a relaxing vacation.

This Fifth Mindfulness Training is about mindful consumption and its powerful effect on our lives. For both of my friends, what seemed at first to be denial was in fact about gaining a greater joy in life and a fuller ability to do what they chose in their lives.

Mindful Exercises

Happiness is within you—the seeds are always there. With practice you can learn to bring feelings of happiness into everything you do and into your relationships. Keep up with your Mindful Morning Meditation, Mindful Memoirs, Mindful Gratitudes, and Mindful Exercises, and continue practicing the Five Mindfulness Trainings.

- For one day, don't just rely on yourself. Ask for what you need or for the support and help you require.
- We are always reflections of others. Look for the values and beauty in each other. Write down ten things you like in a co-worker, family member, or friend. Then write down ten things you like in someone you do not prefer—a hard exercise!
- Watch where you expend unnecessary energy on doing things—speeding through life can be a habit! Remember the old adage, "When you are in a hurry, slow down." Write down five ways you rush through life.
- The next time you are drinking juice or eating an orange, try using it for a meditation. First, really taste the orange or juice, just close your eyes, and maybe you will actually taste an orange for the first time. Sit down at a table and just eat or drink that orange or juice. Then, when your mind starts to protest and say, "This is silly just sitting here and eating an orange and not doing anything else," really start to look deeply into the orange and its journey from an orange seed in the ground to your tummy. Look deeply into everything and everyone that has been connected

with its journey, and you will begin to have a completely new understanding of your orange and our "interbeing" world. Of course, if you don't like oranges, just choose another fruit!

- Take a look at your habits, both the self-nurturing and the destructive ones. Make a list of five positive and destructive habits and what you are going to do to change one of the destructive ones.

- What books or magazines do you read that upset your mind or bring joy to your mind?

- What TV programs or films do you watch that bring peace to your mind or upset your mind?

- What foods do you eat that upset your body? Write about the feelings you have before and after you eat these foods.

- What exercises are you doing that you do not enjoy? What exercises do you enjoy?

- Call a friend who is really supportive of you and go for a walk with that person. Do a walking meditation together—just following your steps and breathing—and then sit down and talk face to face after the walk or sit together drinking tea, doing nothing, or enjoying nature.

- This week, eliminate something superfluous from your life. In fact, eliminate five superfluous items!

- Identify a habit that is destructive to you. Start breaking this habit you don't like by slowly cutting back on it.

- Eat one (family) meal in silence this week. Say a gratitude before you eat.

- Figure out what you do not need in your life, maybe some things you can eliminate from your home or your place of work. Start with one room, one cupboard, one bookcase, or maybe one messy area and ask each item, "Why are you in my life?"

- Pretend your house is on fire and you have fifteen minutes to take anything you want and put it into the trunk of your car—write out the list.
- If your finances are suffering, keep a list for one week of everything you spend money on (and that really means every single item!). At the end of the week see what you can eliminate.
- Notice sources of noise such as radios, television, CD players, traffic, or gatherings, and then try to eliminate one of them from your life this week. Listen for natural sounds, the wind, the birds, and appreciate them.
- Take one of your cravings and eliminate it from your life for the next week. Then try to keep eliminating it for the next twenty-three days. Remember, it takes thirty days to change any habit.

Mindful Memoirs:
Age Twenty-nine to Thirty-five

If you are younger than this, write about how you would like your life to be during these years. Describe the life you would like to be living.

- Take a look at the dysfunctional patterns that may be showing up in your family, friendships, and love life. These are patterns of perceived abandonment, deprivation, subjugation, mistrust, and un-lovability. See how they relate to some of your earlier memoirs.

- Take a look at the other destructive patterns that may be showing up in your life. These could be things like exclusion, vulnerability, perception of failure, perfectionism, and entitlement. These mostly manifest in our working lives or in our community. Again, see how they relate to your earlier years.

- If you were married or had a partner, describe your life together. What activities did you do together and apart? Did you have both mutual and your own friends?

- If you were single, describe your life. Were you single by choice or circumstances? What were the advantages and disadvantages? Were there periods of loneliness? Did you enjoy your independence and freedom?

- If you were single and lived alone or with other people, describe what you liked or disliked about your homes.

- If you lived in an apartment, house, or vacation home during these years write about how you felt about it.

- If you had children, write about how they changed your life. What kind of parent were you in their early years? If you had to do it all over again, what would you do differently?

- What type of education did you choose for your children? What style of discipline did you use? How much time did you spend with your children? What religious or spiritual influences did you have on your children? What connection did you have with your children then?

- If you did not have children, do you regret not having children during this period or not at all?

- What kind of work career did you choose? Did you work

for a salary or were you self-employed? How ambitious were you at this stage of your life? Were you happy doing this work?

- If you had to do it all over again, would you have chosen the same field of work? If not, what would you have chosen?

- How did you work with other colleagues? What did you learn from others and your work experiences at that time? Did you ever leave a job or get fired? How did that feel?

- If you decided to be a homemaker, for whatever reason, how did you enjoy it? Did you find yourself stimulated or bored? Did you manage the household budget monies? Write about your friends, and educational or social activities during this period of your life.

- What was the social, economic, and historical environment like at this period of your life? How did it affect your life? What was the social, economic, and historical environment like for your parents at the same age grouping?

Weekly Check-in

Be kind, compassionate, accepting, and honest with yourself.

- How many days did I do Mindful Meditation?
- How many days did I do Mindful Memoirs?
- How many nights did I do Mindful Gratitudes?
- How many Mindful Exercises did I do?

WITHOUT MY DREAMS

WITHOUT MY PILGRIMAGE

I WOULD HAVE MISSED THIS DREAM

W · E · E · K   S · E · V · E · N

Loving Kindness

How many moments are in a day? How fast life seems to go, if we are not fully present to enjoy each and every moment! Imagine there is a bank that credits your account each morning with $86,400. It carries over no balance from day to day; every evening the bank wipes out any unused amount. What would you do? Why, most of us would draw out every single dollar and cent of course!

The funny thing is, each of us has such an account with the "Moment Bank." Every morning you are credited with 86,400 seconds or moments. However, every night, whatever you have failed to invest is lost. It carries over no balance. It allows no over–draft. If you fail to use the day's deposits, the loss is yours. There's no going back, no borrowing against tomorrow. You must live in the present on today's deposits. Invest it, so as to get from it the utmost in peace, joy, and happiness.

Choosing Freedom

I know that I don't have to die in order to go to hell; I can be there right now, here on Earth! It all begins here in my head and in my mind. So many of us spend so much of our time living in our past or in our future, neither of which exist. And then we live in a kind

Waking up this morning, I smile. Twenty-four brand new hours are before me. I vow to live fully in each moment and to look at all beings with eyes of compassion.

–THICH NHAT NHAH

*We shall not cease
from exploration
And the end of all
our exploring
Will be to arrive
where we started
And know the
place for the first
time.*

—T.S. ELIOT

of "slavery," missing out on the precious present. With each moment, with each breath, we have a choice to live in bondage or to live in freedom. Which do you want?

My mind can "enslave" me when it chooses to churn up the hurts and anger from the past, relive them right now, and then I live in hell. However, I have the choice to change my thoughts in my mind, and when I change my story, my perceptions change. First, I have to recognize what is troubling my mind. When I take the time to meditate upon it, I can begin to understand it. That is what Mindful Memoirs are all about. I must realize that I cannot change anything in the past—I can only begin to heal myself in the present moment! Understanding something leads to acceptance, which in turn begins the process of learning to love myself again.

It has been said that the opposite of slavery is freedom. A friend once told me that she thinks the opposite of slavery is uncertainty. I am not entirely sure I agree with her; however, I do believe that in order to unshackle the chains we place on ourselves, we have to pass through "a veil of uncertainty." If we trust ourselves and personally forgive ourselves, then we can have freedom. With this first small step of acknowledging past hurts, I can start to heal by giving myself loving kindness. Once I have made peace with my past, my attitudes can change. I can begin being responsible for myself right now.

When we trust ourselves enough to forgive the injustices of our past and begin anew, we can start living in the precious present and enjoy living in peace and joy. We can be in heaven on Earth. However, it requires us to remember to stop for a moment, breathe deeply several times, and then come back to what is really happening right now.

REFLECTION: A PEACEFUL SACRED PLACE

Sometimes, when I need to relax or "get away from it all" and calm my mind, I recreate a peaceful place, in my mind, from my childhood. I go to a special place in my mind that feeds and fills me spiritually.

I grew up on a farm in England. Our next-door neighbors all lived a mile or more away from us. Our farm was situated in a very lovely part of Sussex just under the South Downs. My parents had to drive me to neighboring farms so I could spend time interacting and playing with other children. So I learned very early to amuse myself on my own and to enjoy the solitude that my parents' chosen lifestyle gave me. One of the things I loved most was going into the farm's oak tree woods. They were like an enchanted forest to my childish imagination. In the springtime I would go there and pick primroses and bluebells, and in the autumn play in the piles of crisp brown leaves. As there was never any fear at that time of a child being abducted or lost, I was allowed to wander all over the farm by myself.

I was a tomboy who loved tree climbing. I loved to climb as high as I could up into the trees and look at the world from a different viewpoint. One day, I fell out of a rather large tree into a spiky holly bush. I was covered with scratches from its prickly leaves, but otherwise unhurt. I ended up in a small area on the ground inside the holly bush, maybe four feet by four feet, where no leaves or branches grew. As I sat there for a few minutes, dazed by my fall, I realized that my misfortune had

One truly is the protector of oneself; Who else could the protector be? With oneself fully controlled, one gains A mastery that is hard to obtain.

–THE DHAMMAPADA

Whoever shows up are the right people. Whenever it starts is the right time. Whatever happens is the only thing that could have happened. And when it's over, it's over.

–ANGELES ARRIEN

led me to a secret hiding place! This was to become my special sacred place to hide from the outside world.

Over the next few months I returned regularly and brought with me with special items I found around the farm: an old tin can in which I placed wildflowers, some colorful stones, beautiful bird feathers, odd shaped sticks, even special cut-out pictures and a small stool. It became a place where I could still my mind and listen to my inner truth. I could close my eyes, listen to nature and really hear it. I could open my eyes, just stare at nature and really see it. I could smell the rich scent of the bare earth. I felt very safe and secure. After my daily visits I felt more deeply connected to myself. I didn't know it at the time, but I had found a meditation or personal retreat space. I told no one about my secret hiding place, as it was too precious to share with the rest of the world.

We all need a special place to retreat to that is just ours and that nobody else shares with us. It may only be a small shelf or a tiny table. Mine is a small table covered with a precious scarf given by a friend. It has a small statue of a Buddha and a Palm Sunday Cross, two photos—one of myself as a child of about seven and another of my family taken when I was about three. There is also always an ever-changing collection of items such as stones, shells, seeds, leaves, a freshly picked flower, a few written words that touch me, a pretty candle, or some incense. It could be called an altar or just my special space. It touches a part of my personal history, my spiritual ancestors, people in my life, and the present moment. For me, it is a place of gratitude for my family, who are still so much a part of me, and a place of gratitude to our beautiful Earth and all who inhabit it, without which or without whom I could not survive. I have a little stool beside my special place to rest upon and meditate. It is a small wooden meditation bench with the words "Breathe my dear" that I embroidered in yellow upon its pretty purple seat cover.

This special place is somewhere I can go daily to relax and be fully present. It is my special place to sit and stop my monkey mind from its eternal chatter and find peace, stillness, joy, and serenity in the moment. We all need a sacred place like this. It is one of the ways that I use to show love and compassion to myself. It helps feed my spiritual needs. I encourage you to find a special spiritual sanctuary for yourselves. It is one way of "getting away" from our day-to-day routine and responsibilities. Maybe eventually we shall all find that we don't have to "get away" from our homes as often just to find ourselves!

Responsibility Versus Blame

I once read that the opposite of personal responsibility is blame. That definition came as a bit of a shock, for I had always thought that the opposite of responsibility was irresponsibility. But when I thought about it, I realized that I often hear people blaming this, that, or someone else for their problems, instead of taking responsibility for themselves and their own lives. In many ways, this is what the philosophy of mindfulness is all about—personal responsibility and not blaming others for our so-called problems.

*Be the person
you wish to be
in the world.*

–UNKNOWN

Mindfulness is just another word for a clear mind, an awakened mind or being fully conscious. It means cultivating a nonjudgmental awareness of our moment-to-moment experiences. When combined with meditation or quiet prayer time, it helps us with our capacity to be present and to experience our lives in a direct and fuller manner. This way we start to "own" each moment of our own life experiences, whether they are pleasant or unpleasant.

Unfortunately, it is those unpleasant experiences that usually lead us to blame others for our problems. However, research into stress management tells us that most of our mental anguish doesn't come from experiences themselves, but instead, it comes from how we mentally perceive those experiences and handle them. Is it the engine (my mind) in the boat (my body) that powers the boat to move ahead? Or is it the wake (my past) behind the boat that powers it to move ahead? Using a mindful approach to stress and problems allows us to start relating to our experiences with much less fear and anxiety. Then we can begin to develop a more friendly, caring, and responsible attitude towards ourselves as we learn to make different choices about how we relate to these experiences.

The ultimate goal is to fully take on the responsibility for our own thoughts, actions, and feelings, instead of blaming another person or a situation. This means we must be proactive rather than reactive. Learning to stop blaming others forces us to let go of our old patterns and past conditioning, and helps create a feeling of being spacious and awakened. And in the end, we can reconnect with our sense of wholeness, no matter what we are facing!

This approach lets you create peace out of chaos. It reminds me of the Chinese calligraphy for the word "crisis," which is a combination of the symbols for both "danger" and "opportunity." However, the obvious question is, "How does one put mindfulness into practice on a day-to-day basis?" The answer is simple: stop the mind through meditation and by going back to the breath, develop self-understanding through self-reflection and the Mindful Memoirs, and gain a fuller appreciation of life through expressing gratitude.

Life is suffering. This is the First Noble Truth and we don't deny it. But there is an end to suffering. We can shorten the time by noting our own and others' suffering, seeking out the origins of that suffering, and doing something to end that suffering. Through mindfulness, we can see what is feeding our suffering and cut off that source of nourishment.

How to Have a Wonderful Relationship

Most people are looking for a loving "relationship" with someone else. Many people get what they are seeking—the almost unconditional love and understanding of another person. However, what starts out as our need to be loved by another can end up as a "needy relationship." And nobody wants that, because that is when blaming and resentment become issues. And then the relationship is definitely no longer a truly loving and understanding partnership.

So how can we have a loving, understanding, and great relationship with another? Our first responsibility is actually to be able to love ourselves unconditionally. This means to love ourselves fully, accept ourselves fully, even if we sometimes do not understand ourselves fully! When we do this, we can then begin to love another fully, accept another fully, and even if we don't always understand them fully, at least sometimes understand the other person!

Being compassionate with ourselves is sometimes a very hard practice. One of the reasons it is so hard is because we often take

Until you make peace with who you are, you'll never be content with what you have.

–DORIS MORTMAN

on the responsibility for how other people feel. However, when you are not fully responsible for your own feelings, for your own thoughts, and for your own actions, then you are actually being irresponsible to that other person. And that is when you start to blame the other person and feel resentment. Taken further, it leads to upset and anger in your relationships.

We have to learn the difference between being responsible for ourselves and being responsible to others. Responsibility for ourselves and to others is a concept that is very difficult for many of us to understand. I know that for myself, as I grew up in a place and at a time when the accepted norm was that "my prince would arrive in shining armor and we would live happily ever after" and that he would be responsible for me forever! This of course made me believe that someone else was going to be responsible for me and for my happiness. I was also taught that I was responsible for my children. I even thought I was responsible for my children's feelings, thoughts, and actions. It was a great way to take away anyone's self-worth!

Later in life, after years of thinking that someone else was responsible for my happiness, some major predicaments in my life came along, and I had to relearn how to be totally responsible for myself. I also had to relearn how to love and care for myself before all others. I soon realized that my children were perfectly capable of being responsible for themselves and that I was only responsible to them—to love them, to teach them good values, and to accept them totally for who they were. So, to have a great relationship with another we have to first take full ownership and responsibility for our feelings, for our thoughts, and for our actions in any situation, before we can be responsible to another in a relationship. Please reread the last three paragraphs especially noting the "to" and "for" words, they are so important to understand fully.

Thich Nhat Hanh has a beautiful practice for both couples and individuals on the evening of the full moon. It is called the Five Awarenesses and involves repeating together the following in the moonlight:

The Five Awarenesses

- We are aware that all generations of our ancestors and future generations are present in us.
- We are aware of the expectations that our ancestors, our children, and their children have of us.
- We are aware that our joy, peace, freedom, and harmony are the joy, peace, freedom, and harmony of our ancestors, our children, and their children.
- We are aware that understanding is the very foundation of love.
- We are aware that blaming and arguing never help us and only create a wider gap of misunderstanding. Only understanding, trust, and love can help us change and grow.

Personal Accountability

We all come up against circumstances in life that cause us grief. However, it is how we respond to our circumstance that's so important! We have a choice. We can react, feel threatened, blame others for our circumstances, and make excuses. We can have negative thoughts about any circumstance in life and react to it and then our behavior becomes defensive. When this happens we become the "victim of circumstance" and our peace and joy don't

grow at all. We get into the no–growth cycle of blame and resentment. We become victims. Almost all of us fall into this category
from time to time. And some of us live there all of the time, and
then life is not very much fun at all! It certainly is not the life we
love to live.

However, we also have a choice to be proactive when the circumstances in life cause us grief. We can look at any circumstance in life
and respond in a positive manner. When life gives us a thump over
the head with a hammer, there is a reason for it—a blessing hidden
in the hammer. We can take back our power and leadership and be
proactive. This usually takes some creative behavior; however, it can
help us get the life we love to live. We become personally accountable and become accountable for the results in our lives.

So when life hits us over the head with a circumstance that feels
out of our control, we can always choose how we respond to that
circumstance. We can feel threatened and use defensive behavior,
blame others, make excuses for ourselves, and become the victim
of circumstance. Or, we can look at it as an opportunity to practice.

Uni-tasking Versus Multi-tasking

In many ways, living mindfully is ultimately an ongoing quest for
unity. The late Gordon Allport talked about this search for unity
and believed that it was at the heart of all religious or spiritual
inclinations. It is the desire to see the interconnectedness of everything, but it is also the need to be unified with one's self, as well
as the desire to find unity and meaning in both our own life experiences and in the whole universe.

This idea is in many of the world's religions. It is very much like
the Hindu idea of finding God in oneself, in everyone, in every liv-

ing creature, or in everything on this Earth. In Buddhism there is the idea of nonself, the actual physical fact that we are made up of everything from our direct ancestors to the rain and the Earth's minerals in our foods, to atoms in the air that we breathe into our bodies from the atmosphere. We can see we are all a part of everything else and therefore have "no separate self."

All spiritual or religious paths have an emphasis on the right way of living. Hinduism stresses this through Dharma (the Truth or the Living Law) and karma in which we are responsible for our actions and therefore their results. In Islam, God is Creator of the whole universe and absolute unity and power resides in God. The Quran stresses that life on Earth is a test and a preparation for the life to come—again, responsibility for our actions. Taoism (which means "The Way" or course of life) stresses the integral unity of mankind and the natural order of things. In Buddhism, freedom from life's suffering is achieved through understanding and practicing the Four Noble Truths and the Eightfold Path of right understanding, thought, speech, action, livelihood, effort, awareness (mindfulness), and concentration. Again, the emphasis is on responsibility for our own actions.

The one thing that comes out of all this is our personal responsibility in life. This is what the practice of mindfulness is all about and where "uni-tasking" (as opposed to multi-tasking) comes in. So what is uni-tasking? It is when we are doing only one thing at a time and totally concentrating on that, or when we are conscious of only one thought, or when we are mindful of our listening and speaking skills. Or, as my friend Peggy says, mindfulness is the exact opposite of today's busy multi-tasking world where we are supposed to be able to do many things all at once.

The Buddha told a story in which he said that the problem of life

The real voyage of discovery consists not in seeking new landscapes but in having new eyes.

–MARCEL PROUST

or death is in itself the problem of mindfulness. Whether or not one is alive depends on whether one is mindful or not. He said, "A very famous dancer came to perform in a small village. Many people came to see her perform. At the same time a condemned criminal was obliged to cross the village carrying a bowl of oil filled right to the brim. He had to concentrate with all his might to keep the bowl of oil steady, for if he spilled just one drop the soldier behind him had orders to take out his sword and cut off his head." Then he asked, "Do you think the prisoner was able to keep his attention so focused on the bowl of oil that his mind did not stray to take a glace at the dancer, or to look up at the villagers thronging the village streets in case one might bump into him?"

Trust

Trust is perhaps the most essential ingredient in any relationship. And as my relationship with myself is the primary and the most important relationship that I'll ever have (the only relationship that I will live with twenty-four hours of the day for the rest of my lifetime) I know I have to trust myself fully. If I don't trust myself, what happens to my relationship with myself or to my self-esteem? "To thine own self be true," William Shakespeare wrote. This means looking deeply at myself and really knowing what is right for me and then trusting my own truth.

I often say to people who cannot remember my name, "Rub the bottle and the Genie (Jeanie) will come out and grant you a wish!" Perhaps there is more to that statement than I realize! For it is sometimes not easy to trust that still small voice that we hear within ourselves. That's probably why, for many of us, it is not easy to fully trust another person. When I share my inner self, I actually can become very vulnerable. For when I give of myself fully to others, they may not fully understand me. I have to be somewhat brave with the closeness or intimacy that comes from letting someone else into my inner world.

It is the same when others trust me enough to be true to themselves; they may fear there will be a misunderstanding. However, when I have enough faith in myself to be true to myself, it actually stimulates them to reveal themselves more fully. My trust encourages them to trust me, and then their faith allows our relationship to grow so much deeper and stronger.

Faith is a large ingredient of trust, but what is faith? I believe that all we have to do is stop, breathe, quiet our monkey minds, be still, and then allow the answers within us to just come. Then, and this is sometimes the hard part, we have to trust enough that what we are told or what we have heard will truly be our next step. Faith is asking for the help we need from the universe.

What are the other ingredients of trust? One of the elements of trust is dependability. Do I keep my commitments to myself and to others? Openness is another ingredient. Is what I am saying, doing, and feeling congruent? Others know instinctively if I am fudging it and not telling my truth. Am I open with my communication and do I give good feedback to the feelings of others? Good communication in a relationship is of vital importance. Mindful speech and mindful listening are also about trust. If we are going to be truthful then we are also vulnerable, and we can trust that the person we are speaking to will hear us in that same spirit of trust. The last, and perhaps most important element of trust is acceptance. Acceptance is realizing that we are all unique spiritual beings and that we must accept other human beings for who and where they are at, in this moment, right now. After all, who decides whether or

Every blade of grass has its Angel that bends over it and whispers, 'Grow, grow.'

–THE TALMUD

not it is "okay"? Who am I to say what is too big, too small, too much, too little, too straight, too weird, too late, too soon? And whose lens is seeing this?

You need to claim the events of your life to make yourself yours.

–ANNE-WILSON SCHAEF

Like an ability or a muscle, hearing your inner wisdom is strengthened by doing it.

–ROBBIE GASS

REFLECTION: ZEN GOLF

Tiger Woods is an extraordinary golfer. Not only has he a superb natural physical capacity to play the game, but he has a mental and emotional calm. Golfers call this his "head game." I, on the other hand, am not a natural sportswoman. Despite not being particularly good at it, I love the game of golf and I've tried to understand my golf head game as much as I try to understand my life head game.

I was well over forty years of age when my husband decided he wanted to play more of his greatest passion in life. However, he didn't want me to be a golf widow, so he said he'd only play if I joined him. Although I knew nothing about the game, I said I would take up the challenge. And what a challenge it has been.

The next thing I knew, I received a set of golf clubs as my Christmas gift from my over-zealous husband. I didn't know then the difference between a putter and a driver, but I thanked him. Now the game was about to begin.

Golf is one of the most humbling of games. Sometimes it is satisfying, sometimes it is frustrating, and sometimes it is just plain painful. I've learned a lot about my friends through watching the way they play the game. There are the competitive folk who are only satisfied with win/lose, never happy with win/win. They want to win so badly that some are even happy when others are having a horrible game of golf that day. There are the oh-so-serious ones, who play golf as though it was the most important thing in their world. There are the ones who are more interested in having fun with fine company and those whose idea of a good game of golf is only what is for lunch afterwards. There are those who berate themselves every time they make a poor shot. There are those who pressure their partners with their own playing psychology and words. There are those who encourage you and those who don't.

One of the ways to improve the physical side of golf is to practice, something I struggle with. I get bored doing the same thing over again. Similarly, in life I am often drawn to the distraction, novelty, or buzz. In golf, as soon as I notice myself being distracted, I stop and take a deep breath. By the time I have taken my second deep breath, I feel more relaxed. I stop staring at the ball or the hole and instead let myself take in the whole of my surroundings and the beauty of the moment. Sometimes, instead of spending hours on the driving range or the putting green, I use mental movements or visualization. This has helped my game around the green immensely and it appears that often these days I drive the ball just where I know I am capable of hitting it. However, forgetfulness is my greatest enemy. I often forget to visualize or concentrate before driving, chipping, or putting the ball, just as often in life I rush in, forgetting to take a moment first to be mindful of how I am entering a space.

You must first be who you really are, then do what you need to do, in order to have what you want.

–SHAKTI GAWAIN

*Be really whole
and all things will
come to you.*

–LAO-TZU

Another thing I do is use the time on the golf course as a walking meditation from shot to shot. Instead of allowing my mind to worry about my game or anything else, I just walk and follow my breath. This allows me to enjoy the beauty of nature all around me, rather than stewing over a missed shot. I truly believe the games of golf and life are played mostly in our minds. As in life, I try to play the game moment-by-moment. If I live in the past, tormenting myself about my last awful shot or worrying about the next one, then I miss out on the wonders of nature or the company of the wonderful folk I am playing with.

Gratitude goes a long way to making this game so much more beautiful. I am just so grateful to have the free time and resources available to play this game that requires both. I am grateful that I have the energy to be able to walk the eighteen holes. I am often so thankful that I can still see the ball and the beautiful scenery surrounding the golf course. More than any particular score or shot, I enjoy the peace and joy in the present moment.

I always make sure that I take a deep (and non-noisy) breath before I swing at the ball. This not only relaxes my muscles, but also allows me to fully be aware of only my golf swing, and synchronizes body and mind. It gives me mastery over that moment. Then, when I breathe again, the next moment has arrived! And, just as in life, I can always begin anew in the next moment. So each golf shot is just another golf shot. I do my best, and if it doesn't work out some days, I am not too upset by it, because there is always the next game or day. By being mindful, I protect myself from becoming upset and unhappy, and by being fully controlled in my mind, I gain mastery over my life.

Mindful Exercises

The best gift you can give another is to choose to be responsible for yourself. Do not put the burden of your needs on someone else's doorstep. This week, write down how you are being responsible *for* others in small ways and in the larger picture and also write down how you can change that to being responsible to them.

It's your life, so gain the support and love of those closest to you; it can make an incredible difference. Mix with messy people and your life could become messy. Mix with happy people and you'll learn about happiness. This week, write down who is adding to your life and who is taking away your energy. Start by spending more time with the former and less with the latter.

I hope that some of the following ideas may help you lead a stress-free life at home and also at work. They seem so very simple (maybe too simple), however, please give at least one a try each day this coming week. I guarantee you'll see the difference it makes to lead a more aware or mindful life. The simplicity of the teaching is that when we walk we only walk, when we talk we only talk, and when we eat we only eat. Let your mind and your actions "be" totally at one with the other person. Many people may say, "So what is new? I have heard all of these ideas before." That might be true, but ask yourself: "Do I actually practice them?"

- Rule number one is always to keep things as simple as possible.
- Breathe deeply and often.
- Begin and end the day with prayer, meditation, or reflection.
- Let Mother Nature nurture.
- Carve out an hour a day for solitude.
- Stop trying to please everybody.
- Don't squander precious resources, time, creative energy, or emotion.
- Cultivate gratitude in each moment.
- Never make a promise you can't keep.
- Remember that happiness is a living emotion.
- Complete everything.
- Set aside one day a week for total rest and renewal.

Write down, in very large print, "My life is my practice." Post these words in a place where you will see them often. You know that life only happens in the present moment. You know that your thoughts lead to your actions. Actions change you.

Mindful Memoirs: Age Thirty-six to Forty-nine

Write only about memories from this age grouping. If you are younger than this, write about how you would like your life to be during these years.

- How well do you fit into your environment—at home, work, and socially?

- Do you fully express yourself by using your natural gifts, attributes, talents, and skills?
- What are you passionate about in this time period? What are your beliefs and values?
- What makes you unique?
- What do you contribute to others and your community?
- Write about what money really means to you during this period of your life.
- Write about what family really means to you during this period of your life.
- Describe what spirituality really means to you at this time.
- Describe what freedom really means to you at this time.
- What are your dreams and ambitions at this time?
- Write about the man or woman you admire most who is in this age grouping now.

Weekly Check-in

Be kind, compassionate, accepting, and honest with yourself.

- How many days did I do Mindful Meditation?
- How many days did I do Mindful Memoirs?
- How many nights did I do Mindful Gratitudes?
- How many Mindful Exercises did I do?

A CHORUS OF TREE FROGS

NEIGHBORS IN A SMALL COMMUNITY

EACH ALONE

W · E · E · K   E · I · G · H · T

Community

My dear teacher Thich Nhat Hanh says that each week we need a Lazy Day. This is a "do nothing day." And what a treat it is too! Kobi Yamada, Compendium's young top executive and the author of several books, helps managers at large companies such as Microsoft, Starbucks, and The Gap communicate their vision and mission in a way designed to retain employees, build company loyalty, and provide a better quality of life. He had a similar idea and calls them Receiving Days. He says, "Be good to yourself. If you don't take care of your body, where will you live?"

All religions offer the idea of weekly days of rest; however, in our fast-paced and over-stressed world—between work, children, family, and other commitments—it is difficult for most of us to find time to practice this. What a complete and total luxury and blessing it is to spend a day doing nothing but receiving, partaking in a sitting meditation, a walking meditation, some deep relaxation, and then maybe indulging in something that we really love. It is a day to spend some time by oneself in silence. It is a day to treat and re-treat ourselves, a day of renewal. Some people can pay large amounts of money to go to a spa for a couple of hours or a retreat center for a weekend, but you can get the same benefits right in your own home. Do not give up on this idea because you don't have a whole day. Even an hour a week of unstructured time, devoted completely to relaxation and awareness, will make a huge difference in your life.

Lazy Day

Here are some ideas of the numerous ways to re-treat or to spend your weekly lazy day. As a retiree I am fortunate to be able to choose a whole day each week for mindfulness. I have chosen Mondays as my lazy day or day of mindfulness, in part because I like the sound. "Mindful Mondays" are now a part of my weekly routine.

Here are some ideas of how to spend your lazy time, whether it's an hour or a whole day:

Breathe. Slow down. Go for a walk in nature. Meditate on the beach or on a park bench. Enjoy solitude. Give gratitude for your life. Write in your Mindful Memoirs or your journal. Enjoy the now. Have a long relaxing bath. Light some candles. Play some relaxing music. Have a massage. Take care of your skin by using a nourishing body oil or lotion. Watch a sunrise or sunset from a nearby place of beauty. Enjoy walking in the rain. Chant. Walk a labyrinth. Visit a favorite bookstore or music store. Make an appreciation phone call to a friend. Dance in your living room. Talk to someone you don't know. Don't worry, be happy. Don't answer the phone all day. Have a picnic in nature or at home on the floor. Enjoy wind chimes and bells. Play. Sing. Enjoy a special treat. Be kind to yourself. Practice mindfulness all day long. It can be even more challenging than on a day with planned activities.

Retreats

Many of us do not feel we have the financial opportunity or time to take a retreat away from our regular lives, even for a night. For many of us, there is very little time, but even one night of the year on a retreat for yourself can make a huge difference. This can be done in so many ways—only you know the best one for you. Try to make an appointment with yourself early in each new year for this special time with yourself. Sometimes we tend to procrastinate with the very things we need the most.

One of the best ways to commit to taking this time for yourself is, paradoxically, to have a group or community of a few others who support and encourage you. Thich Nhat Hanh tells a story of a pebble being thrown into the river of life. He says, of course it will sink. However, he tells us that if we build a boat, we can pile many pebbles into that boat and then this boat can float down the river. Our community, our group, is this boat.

This story illustrates that often it is very difficult to practice mindfulness alone; however, if we share our difficulties and our victories with a group of like-minded individuals, it is so much easier. Even if you do not know the long-term direction of your group, you can form for just the eight weeks of this Mindful Way journey. Perhaps, after that, you will stay together as a community or you may find at least one other individual who wants to continue following this practice of mindfulness. It is important that you and your friends set up agreed upon ground rules and assumptions at the start. An information sheet that we give all our friends to read as soon as they arrive at the Mindful Way centers is included in Appendix C. Please feel free to adapt it for your own use.

In solitude we give passionate attention to our lives, to our memories, to the details around us.

–VIRGINIA WOOLF

*The beginning is
always today.*

–MARY WOLLSTONECRAFT

REFLECTION: WONDERFUL WORDS

John Davison Rockefeller gave money away from the moment he started to earn a living. And he gave away more than the usual tithing of ten percent. He was a devout Baptist who gave monies not only to his church but also to those who really needed it. In 1859, he gave a man enough money to buy his wife out of slavery. His son, John D. Rockefeller, Jr., inherited his sense of philanthropy. He has said, "I believe that every right implies a responsibility; every opportunity, an obligation; every possession, a duty."

Responsibility to me means our own personal responsibility, and never blaming others for our un-skillfulness. We know that with all opportunities and possessions there are always obligations and duties, and the Five Mindfulness Trainings encourage us to leave our world a better place and our relationships in greater harmony.

Rockefeller, Jr.'s words continue: "I believe in the dignity of labor, whether with head or hand; that the world owes no man a living but that it owes every man an opportunity to make a living." If we are physically and mentally able, there are ample opportunities in this world to work. If we are willing to start from a place that suits our abilities and skills, work hard, then more opportunities do open up.

"I believe that thrift is essential to well-ordered living and that economy is a prime requisite of a sound financial structure, whether in government, business, or personal affairs." As human beings we always want more, rather than being satisfied with "enough." In the Samyutta Nikaya I, 117, an early Buddhist text, it says, "Were there a mountain all made of gold, double that would not be enough to satisfy a single man: know this and live accordingly."

Rockefeller continues, "I believe that truth and justice are fundamental to an enduring social order. I believe in the sacredness of a promise, that a man's word should be as good as his bond; that character—not wealth or power or position— is the supreme worth." The Fourth Mindfulness Training of mindful speech could be applied here, committing only to what we are able to do and fulfill. For our actions do speak so much louder than words. "I believe that the rendering of useful serv- ice is the common duty of mankind and that only in the puri- fying fire of sacrifice is the dross of selfishness consumed and the greatness of the human soul set free." It certainly is greater to give than to receive; generosity is the basis of the Second Mindfulness Training. The spirit feels alive when we do give. If only we can relieve the suffering of one person in the morn- ing and bring joy to another in the afternoon, our day feels better. And this doesn't usually involve any great sacrifice!

"I believe in an all-wise and all-loving God, named by whatever name, and that the individual's highest fulfillment, greatest happiness, and widest usefulness are to be found in living in harmony with his will." These are such releasing words, allowing us not to waste precious energy over things that we cannot control.

"I believe that love is the greatest thing in the world; that it alone can overcome hate; that right can and will triumph over might." If we could only remember this at all times, what a different world we would live in! However, we know that the only person in the world we can change is ourselves. The amazing thing is, when we do change our attitudes everyone else seems to change! Start with loving and being responsible for yourself, and love will definitely triumph over might.

Ask, and it shall be given to you; seek, and ye shall find; knock and it shall be opened unto you.

–MATTHEW 7:7

The Four Mantras

For the longest time I had the following four short sentences on my refrigerator door. I am still trying to bring them into my life more frequently. I am still working at bringing them into my daily practice where I know they can heal others.

The Four Mantras

"Darling, I am here for you."
"Darling, I know you are there, and I am very happy."
"Darling, I know you suffer. That's why I am here for you."
"Darling, I suffer, please help."

I'd like to tell you about Thich Nhat Hanh's practice of the Four Mantras. It's a practice you can do every day. He says,

It's very pleasant and it's easy. A mantra is a magic formula. Every time you pronounce a mantra, you can transform the situation right away; you don't have to wait. You learn to recite it when the time is appropriate and what makes it effective is your mindfulness and concentration. A mantra doesn't need to be said in Sanskrit or Tibetan; we use our own language.

We practice the first mantra, because when you love someone you have to offer him or her the best you have, and that is your true presence. We practice the second mantra to acknowledge the presence of the person we love. What makes this mantra effective is that we first establish our own presence. Often we are too busy day after day to recognize the one we love. But when you are loved by someone, whether you are young or less young, you need the other person to recognize that you are there.

We use the third mantra when the one we love is suffering. When you suffer, you want the person you love to be aware of your suffering—that's very natural. Even before we have done anything, the other person feels some relief because they know we are aware of their suffering. We say the fourth mantra when we are suffering. When we suffer and we believe the one who caused our suffering is someone we love very much, our tendency is for our pride to be hurt and we don't want to see or be touched by the other person. This is very human. We want to show that we don't need them. You are so sure your suffering comes from him or her, but can you be sure? You may have a wrong perception. This mantra is the most difficult to utter. We have to train ourselves for some time. But it is very important

Creativity occurs in the moment, and in the moment we are timeless.

–JULIA CAMERON

that we say it. When we love each other, we need each other. In true love, there is no room for pride.

These four short sentences can heal very deep wounds. They are sentences that are sometimes tough to say to someone who is truly suffering. They are four sentences that, when used with the utmost of sincerity, can help one move past a very painful moment or situation. Said with complete authenticity, these words can allow those of us who are suffering to open ourselves up to looking deeply into what is really troubling us and understanding ourselves better. That is what this spiritual path we are all walking is really about. We must understand ourselves deeply, so that we may then begin to understand others. After all, the practice of deep understanding is the practice of deep love.

REFLECTION: THE ZEN OF ISLAND LIVING

My favorite book is *A Gift from the Sea* by Anne Morrow Lindbergh, written in 1955. The friend who gave it to me wrote inside the cover, "Jeanie, this book has told me many secrets, and you will understand and appreciate them." This is true; I can go to any page and find something that is of significance in my life. Since that time I have bought and given away dozens of copies of this book to many women throughout the world. It also has told them many secrets. The world has totally changed since she wrote the book, however, the wisdom of her words has not changed one bit.

In a chapter called "A Few Shells" she talks about greedily collecting lots of shells when she first arrived on the island. But she says we cannot collect all the shells on the beach and bring them home. In fact, she feels it is better to collect only a few, or even just one beauty, so that it is set apart and ringed by space—just like an island. As she says, when objects or people are framed in space, their beauty will bloom.

On the islands of Bermuda we have only a little space. However, as Anne Morrow Lindbergh writes, "Paradoxically, in this limited area, space has been forced upon me. The geographical boundaries, the physical limitations, the restrictions on communication, have enforced a natural selectivity. Island living selects for us in many ways, but in a natural and non-artificial way.

"The island selects strangers who have been chosen by an accident of time to live within the confines of this space with me. I am with people I might never have chosen to be my neighbors, however life has chosen them. And what jewels it has given me."

As we all come together on the celestial island called Earth, we have to stretch ourselves to understand each other, and in the process, we ourselves are stretched more fully. We cannot always select the people who come into our lives, but from these unselected folk we can find great enrichment. There are the interesting people and the people we find less interesting; there is quality not quantity; there is slowness not speed; also there are not so many distractions or opportunities. There is simplicity of living that allows us a true awareness of life, a truly mindful life. There is a great balance of physical, mental, and spiritual. There is time to communicate with others. There is time for solitude. And it helps us to understand the great interbeing of life.

Walking for Peace

One of the most bonding things you can do with a Mindful Way group or any mindful community you create, is to walk together in peace. In the group that I am part of, we walk together at least once a month. We do it for the two reasons. One, to become peace, to receive the peace we need by walking in a beautiful garden or park where Mother Nature nourishes us and brings balance and life to our minds and hearts when we are open to her presence.

Second, we walk to restore peace within ourselves, to overflow with peace, sharing it with each other and with the world.

All around the world mindfulness practitioners are walking slowly, in silence, with no banners, chanting, or polarizing confrontations—to practice peace, to walk in peace with every step, to witness peacemaking, and build peace by being alive and steady. They are doing it step by step. They are walking to offer compassion, to learn and share that:

- Love is possible as a genuine way of life, even in the presence of rage and fear.
- Violence in any form is a tragedy that stops all of us from living and sharing a life of harmony and abundance.

We walk for ourselves.
We walk for everyone always, hand in hand.
Walk and touch peace every moment.
Walk and touch happiness every moment.
Each step brings a fresh breeze.
Every step makes a flower bloom under our feet.
Kiss the Earth with your feet.
Print on the Earth your love and happiness.
The Earth will be safe.

–THICH NHAT HANH

- Coming together to embody peace can restore our hope and vision.
- Peace building is choosing to refrain from dehumanizing any person or group.
- True and sustainable peace is a process and can be created by peaceful means.

The slow pace and the silence of our walking can help us to step into the source of understanding and compassion within us and hold everyone with care. Many of us wear white on our walks. White clothing is a symbol of our peaceful intentions. Wearing white started in Jerusalem, where it is dangerous for any large group to gather without some clear sign of peaceful intent. By wearing white we express our common intention with those who share this practice in places that are not safe.

We finish the monthly peace walk with an interfaith prayer of gratitude for life and to share our aspirations for world peace. "Love makes no comparisons. And gratitude can only be sincere if it is joined to understanding. We offer thanks to our Creator that in us all things will find their freedom. Let our gratitude make room for all who will escape with you; the sick, the weak, the needy and afraid, and those who mourn a seeming loss or feel apparent pain, who suffer cold or hunger, or who walk the way of hatred and the path of death. We thank our Creator for one thing alone, that we are separate from no living thing, and therefore one with him/her."

Diverse communities, including Israelis and Palestinians, have used this practice to build community and create mindfulness and peace. It is a fitting note on which to end your eight-week journey of *A Mindful Way*, because all of the information, ideas, and practices in this book require walking the talk. Take each step in mind-

Do not weep; do not wax indignant. Understand.

–BARUCH SPINOZA

Stop thinking and talking about it and there is nothing you will not be able to know.

–ZEN PROVERB

fulness. It is all about daily practice. Just taking the time to follow the simple steps of Mindful Meditation, Mindful Memoirs, and Mindful Gratitudes each day and each week, will transform your life. I hope that by the time you have reached this paragraph, you have already found this to be true.

With courage you will dare to take risks, have the strength to be compassionate and the wisdom to be humble. Courage is the foundation of integrity.

–KESHAVAN NAIR

REFLECTION: BELLS OF MINDFULNESS

One Easter, I was in Toronto, Canada, visiting some of my family, and I decided I would go to church on Easter Sunday. Although a student of the Unity Church for many years, I opted for a beautiful little Anglican church close to where I was staying. I arrived to find the congregation singing a truly beautiful hymn and because the church was bursting at its seams, I sat in the side chapel. I immediately felt at home looking at the little side altar decorated with spring flowers and the magnificent stained glass windows surrounding me. It brought back many memories of my Anglican Catholic childhood. Then, all of a sudden, the whole congregation began to ring little bells, something totally new for me. I laughed with delight. They were ringing bells of mindfulness.

In the Thich Nhat Hanh's tradition, temple bells are used to remind us to stop, smile, and to breathe. In stopping, we find our true center, the island of peace that is within us all. My Zen teacher teaches his students to use bells of mindfulness to come back to themselves many times during the day. The Bible also says: "Be still and know we are God." The bells being rung during that Easter morning Anglican service reminded me of my Zen practice of coming back to the breath, smiling, and enjoying the present moment. It was so wonderful to have an unexpected reminder of the interbeing of us all and of all world religions.

In everyday life, we can use many bells of mindfulness to come back to ourselves, to stop, to breathe, and to smile. I call these moments "mini-meditations." It could be the sound of a dog barking, the telephone ringing, the chime of the microwave, an emergency vehicle with its frantic ringing, the horn of a friendly driver beeping hello, streetcar bells clanging, church bells chiming, the computer beep letting us know we have email, a breeze crossing our cheek, or a shaft of sunlight touching us.

In life we can all find our own "bells of mindfulness" that can help us come back to ourselves, stop, breathe, and smile. We do not have to stop for long to find peace in life, we can have it right now with our next breath.

On that Easter weekend I also had the privilege of meeting my future daughter-in-law's parents. At one point Angela's father, Bruno, told me that he was interested in meditation and in leading a less stressful and a more peaceful life. I went out and bought two books, *The Miracle of Mindfulness* and *Peace Is Every Step*, both by Thich Nhat Hanh. These are two beginners' books in the practice of living mindfully or in living in the present moment. When we went for Easter dinner at their lovely home, I gave Bruno my gifts. The next morning when I called to thank them for the day, he said, "I have started to read

All decisions, whatever the outcomes, were simply a way of exploring life.

–GERRY FEWSTER

the books and I am breathing and smiling." Such a simple practice and yet it's so hard for all of us to remember that peace is only one breath away! It was just another bell of mindfulness for me.

Mindful Exercises

- Write out the names of teachers you would like to study with or hear give a lecture. Then take the next step towards studying with them or hearing them speak.
- Write out ways you could practice mindfulness while exercising, be it during yoga, dancing, tennis, golf or whatever exercise your enjoy.
- Join a class or meet up with someone else who enjoys the same hobby as you.
- Spend an unstructured day or hour in mindfulness, a lazy day.
- Spend a day in nature.
- Have a day or weekend retreat in your own home.
- Dance for a half an hour. Create your own dance.
- Notice where you expend unnecessary energy. Speeding through life can be a habit. Remember the adage: when you are in a hurry, slow down.
- Take time to acknowledge yourself—to receive your own praise—for everything that you do during one day this week.
- Smile and say hello to everyone you meet for one day.

- Say NO to as many things as you say YES to for one day.
- Do a five–minute laughing meditation for three mornings this week.
- Make sure you have one night this week that you go to bed by 9 p.m.
- Take a walking meditation every morning instead of doing a sitting meditation.
- If possible to arrange, leave work one hour earlier than you usually do and see if you can get the same amount of work completed.
- Write about the three most painful experiences in your life. See what gifts or benefits came from these situations.
- Form a support group (even if it is only with one other person). If you already have a Mindful Way Group, schedule a retreat together and talk about the how to continue your support of each other.
- Make a list of people who do not truly support you.
- Write about what your biggest issue is or has been. If you don't know what it is, ask other people.

Mindful Memoirs: Age Fifty to Seventy and Over

If you are younger than this age grouping, write about how you would like your life to be during these years. Or you could go back to the other chapters and adapt the questions from earlier age groups.

- How do you help other people during this time of your life? How do other people help you?

- What sayings have great meaning to you?
- What do you love most about the place where you now reside? If you could live anywhere, where would you choose?
- What do you feel proud of?
- What really inspires you?
- What does retirement really mean to you?
- If you had a million dollars, what would you do with it?
- What are ten things that are important to you now, and ten things that are no longer important?
- What was the best gift you ever received?
- What are three things you wish you had done in your life?
- What changes have you seen in your lifetime? How you would change the world?
- When was the saddest day of your life and the happiest day of your life?
- What do most people not know about you?
- What do you hope people say about you?
- What will be written in your obituary?
- How will the world look in fifty years?
- Where have you traveled in your life and where do you wished you had traveled?
- Do you consider yourself to be traditional, modern, or unconventional?
- What has really changed from your childhood to your adulthood?
- What is your all–time favorite book? How can you liken that to some of your values?
- What are your strengths?
- Your oldest friend is...Write about him or her.

- In your free time, you like or would like to…
- What role has spirituality played in your life?
- What are you tolerant and intolerant of?
- How do you feel about the environment?
- What do you think about when you talk about love?
- What does independence mean to you?
- If you could pass on only one recipe for life, this would be…
- Your secrets are…
- What do you need to feel secure?
- Something you have always wanted to have is…
- If you could be another person for a day, who would you want to be?
- Your greatest happiness is…
- Write about someone you haven't spoken to in ten years.
- What are some of the thoughts about marriage or part-nership that you would pass on to others?
- What volunteer work have you been involved in?
- What are some of the favorite stories that have been hand-ed down by your family?
- Write about your health.
- What are some of the technological changes that have been beneficial in your lifetime?
- If you are a grandparent, how do you enjoy this role?
- What new retirement activities are you involved in?
- If you have lost a partner to death or divorce, how are you affected by loneliness? What adjustments have you had to make?
- If you have children, do they still live with you? If they do not, how often do they visit?

- How are you managing financially?
- What advice would you pass on to your children and grandchildren about life, raising children, spirituality, or getting along with other people?
- Do you see your parents differently now that you are older?
- What anniversaries, birthdays, and holidays stand out in your memory?
- Who are some of the people who have most influenced your life?
- Of all the places you have been, which holds the fondest memories?
- Do you have any regrets about your life?
- What would you change in your life?
- Are you pleased with how your life turned out?
- Are you afraid of becoming a burden or having to go into a nursing or old age home?
- If you have lost any of my parents or siblings, how do you feel about this?
- What are your plans for the future? Do you look forward or backwards in your thinking?
- Are you in contact with old friends? Who are those closest to you right now?

Weekly Check-in

Be kind, compassionate, accepting, and honest with yourself.

- How many days did I do Mindful Meditation?
- How many days did I do Mindful Memoirs?
- How many nights did I do Mindful Gratitudes?
- How many Mindful Exercises did I do?
- How much of the Mindful Way course as a whole did I complete?
- Did I get what I was hoping to get out of these eight weeks?
- How did these eight weeks compare with my life before these eight weeks?

OPAL SEAS

PINK OLEANDERS

A MID-ATLANTIC JEWEL

APPENDIXES

Weekly Group Facilitation Guidelines

I t is my sincere hope that within the safety of your Mindful Way Group you will find the joy, freedom, peace, and self-love to move forward into the present moment, rather than live in the past which has already gone or the future that doesn't exist.

Give the course your full effort for eight weeks and it will give you back your mind.

*Leave only foot-
prints behind.*

–SIGN ON LOWER BAY,
BEQUIA, WEST INDIES

Week One

Prior to the first meeting, make sure *all* the group members have read Week One of *A Mindful Way*. This meeting will give everyone the opportunity to understand both this chapter and the overall methodology of the course book. Ask the person who first organized your group to facilitate this first meeting.

Notes for Facilitator

- Have the room set up with a circle of chairs or cushions on the floor.
- Begin in silence. At this meeting start by having everyone sit or lie down quietly in a relaxed position with his or her eyes closed. Then ask everyone to spend the next ten minutes concentrating on silent "tummy breathing." The facilitator could

ring a small bell to mark the beginning and end of the silent session.

■ Introductions: Sit in a circle and have everyone introduce himself or herself by sharing both their name and one reason why they want to do this course. Suggest that this is a time for mindful speech and mindful listening. Allow only one person to speak at a time, while everyone else practices mindful listening. Suggest that each person spend no more than one to two minutes talking. There is no feedback.

■ Housekeeping: Have a brief group discussion as to when and where to meet. Decide upon a place (often the home of each week's facilitator) and a regular day and time (two to three hours) for your group meetings. Ask everyone to arrive ten minutes early, so that the group can start on time. Ask that when members come each week to sit in silence as the group is getting settled. So much can happen throughout the course of a week, so taking a few moments to quietly come into the space can be very helpful in bringing everyone's total presence into the group energy. Remind the group that if anyone is going to be late, to please call the facilitator. If for some reason someone has to miss a meeting, they could call ahead and let the facilitator know so the group may be informed.

■ Facilitators: Each group member could try to take on the role of facilitator for at least one week. The purpose of this is to help empower each individual (it is a great mindfulness exercise) by giving them experience in leading a group. For some it will be old hat, but remember that it may be frightening to others. The goal is not to make it painful, but rather to be open, to stretch our limits a little, and to have fun. The group is there to support everyone, so hopefully nobody will become overly concerned with this aspect.

- Create a course schedule: Establish a facilitator for the first seven weeks. Week Eight could be a silent day of mindfulness. Finally, another time could be arranged soon after the eighth week to have a potluck meal and celebration together.

- What to bring to each weekly meeting: Everyone should bring their copy of *A Mindful Way*, their Mindful Memoirs file, a pen, and paper.

- Emphasize safety and support: This is a non-competitive, process-oriented group where the focus is on the journey, the present moment, while learning appreciation for yourself and each other along the way. Develop a safe place to share challenges as well as successes. Create an environment where all are free to express their authentic selves and speak from their hearts, while addressing the different issues that will help you all move forward on your paths to greater awareness. One of the strongest components for group safety is the collective participation and commitment of each member. This requires that everyone attend each week and that everyone comes prepared, having done the next chapter's reading and exercises, meditations, Mindful Memoirs, and Mindful Gratitudes.

- Confidentiality: A strong component of *A Mindful Way* is uncovering parts of our lives that have been clogged up. We blocked them because they were too painful to address. This course offers us a new beginning, a place past the blocks as we begin to acknowledge our pain, grieve our losses, and take tiny steps toward opening ourselves to our true nature. Whatever is shared in the group stays there. Confidentiality is a strong requirement for feeling safe. Please do not discuss things that went on during the group meeting with friends or family, and respect the confidentiality of group members by not mentioning names or identifying them in any way.

- Respectful and mindful speech/feedback: This means no criticism. What you are undertaking requires tremendous courage. We grow only in an environment of safety, trust, encouragement, and support. Keep your speech focused and listen mindfully.

- Signing a Mindful Way Contract: At the first meeting have everyone sign the contract below. Copy it and read it out loud as a group. Making a group commitment is very encouraging and supportive.

A Mindful Way Contract

I _____ , understand that I am undertaking an intensive encounter with my own awareness. I commit myself fully to the group for the duration of the course.

I _____ , commit to reading a chapter a week, to Mindful Morning Meditation, writing Mindful Memoirs, and expressing daily Mindful Gratitudes.

I _____ , further understand that this course will raise some issues and emotions for me to deal with.

Therefore I commit myself to excellent self-care, adequate sleep, diet, exercise, and pampering for the duration of the course.

_____ , (signature)

_____ , (witnessed by)

_____ (date)

■ The Power of Commitment: Read aloud together the following two quotes:

> "Until one is committed, there is hesitancy, the chance to draw back. Concerning all acts of initiative and creation, there is one elementary truth— the ignorance of which kills countless ideas and splendid plans—the moment one definitely commits oneself, then providence moves too. All sorts of things occur to help one that would never otherwise have occurred. A whole stream of events, issues, and decisions, raising in one's favor all manner of unforeseen incidents and meetings and material assistance, which no one could have dreamed would have come their way...."
> —Goethe

> "Whatever you can do or dream, you can begin. Boldness has genius, power and magic in it. Begin it now..."
> —Unknown

■ On Your Own at Home: Choose the Mindful Exercises that you are drawn to, as well as those that you think may be most challenging to you, as there is a lot to learn from those. Spend at least fifteen minutes on Morning Meditation (twenty is better) then write a minimum of two pages of Mindful Memoirs each morning. Also choose a quote, or quotes, from the chapter that appeal to you and bring it in for your weekly check-in. At night before you go to bed, write your Mindful Gratitudes in a special Gratitude Journal.

Weeks Two to Seven

- Arrive in silence and settle into your space.
- Meditation: The facilitator leads group in fifteen minutes of sitting meditation. Have a little bell to sound at the beginning and end of the meditation. Breathe in and out three times before you start to get yourself grounded. "Wake up" the bell by giving it a little "hello" tap. Then invite (sound) the bell three times, breathing in and out three times in between each sound. Then silently say this guided meditation while you follow your breathing. With your in-breath use the keyword "In" and with your out-breath use the keyword "Out." Then switch to "Deep," "Slow," etc. Never force your breath, just observe it. In the light of your awareness, it will naturally grow deeper and slower.

Breathing in, I know I am breathing in.
Breathing out, I know I am breathing out.
In/Out (wait 2 minutes)

Breathing in, I breathe deeply.
Breathing out, I breathe slowly.
Deep/Slow (wait 2 minutes)

Breathing in, I breathe calmly.
Breathing out, I breathe easily.
Calm/Ease (wait 2 minutes)

Breathing in, I smile.
Breathing out, I release.
Smile/Release (wait 2 minutes)

Breathing in, I know this is the present moment.
Breathing out, I know this is my only moment.
Present Moment/Only Moment (wait 2 minutes)

Breathing in I know this is the present moment.
Breathing out I know this is a wonderful moment.
Present moment/wonderful moment (wait 2 minutes)

After the meditation, wake up the bell again with a tap. Then invite it to sound two times with just one in-breath between the two sounds. Give everyone time to stretch and return to his or her sitting places.

- Check-in: Have each person say their name and how they are feeling in one word, and then ask them to choose one or two quotes from the week's chapter that spoke to them. Read the quotes to the group and tell why they have meaning for you right now. Then tell the group about any totally aware or conscious events that you have experienced during the week.

- Move into pairs: The facilitator reads the following: "Take turns so that each of you can discuss for fifteen minutes the Mindful Memoirs and Exercises you did during the week. Share anything about how it was for you, challenges, what you found difficult, what you really related to, what new awarenesses and insights you may have discovered, and what you had fun with. While one partner is sharing, the other partner is only listening in silence, and that means no interrupting! Do not rustle papers, read from your own notes, or think of what you are going to say. Please be a mindful, respectful, nonjudgmental, and active listener. Establish eye contact at all times.

"This is a time for each of you to see and be seen, speak,

and be heard. Many of us have never really had that in our lives—someone paying absolute attention to what we are saying, feeling, or thinking. This may make you feel uncomfortable, because many of us are not accustomed to being listened to and honored in this way. Breathe. Take it in. It's okay. And again, if you're listening, just listen. No advice giving, no comments, no feedback. Respect each other's boundaries. Do not ask questions about why they feel this way or that way. The facilitator acts as the timekeeper and lets the group pairs know when their two sets of fifteen minutes are up. When each fifteen–minute session is over, thank the other person for listening. After thirty minutes, it will be time to take a break.

"If you're doing the sharing, try to come from your heart and allow yourself to feel your feelings. It's okay, whatever you are feeling. And try not to judge yourself if your partner has totally opposite feelings about the same issues. We are all at different places along our path and have had very different experiences and will have different responses to the lessons. They are all okay. Please be kind to yourself. This is one of the things this course is here to teach you. Please choose a different partner each week."

- Break: Break for a drink and snack (for fifteen minutes). This can either be a silent break or a time to mindfully socialize using the skills of deep listening and mindful speech that you have just practiced.
- Fifteen to thirty minute exercise: The facilitator finds and leads an exercise that relates to the chapter, (or see Appendix B for some group exercise ideas). You may also want to select areas of significance for you from the chapter and create an

exercise to promote any or all of the following: a discussion with deeper exploration of the issues presented, interest, insight, knowledge, or joy. Or use one of the weekly exercises to do as a group and discuss.

- Final circle: Go around the circle with each person saying one or two sentences.
- Song or poem from the facilitator: End your evening with a song or music played from a CD. The person facilitating that week chooses a mindful song or a short piece of music, or reads a poem, a prayer, or anything that represents that week's chapter. You can write one or choose one from another source. Make enough copies for each member to take one home. It is a simple gift.
- Leave in silence and return home mindfully in silence.

Week Eight

By the end of your eight weeks together you will likely feel very close to one another, having shared both tears and laughter. It is for this reason that you need to make your closure as special as possible. These are a few ideas for ending your group's sessions, but feel free to think of other ways you would like to have closure.

- A special day of mindfulness, or a morning, or afternoon, or evening of silent mindfulness together. Each of you may bring a potluck meal. The time can consist of sitting meditation, deep relaxation, mindful walking meditation, and a mindful silent meal together.
- Before the celebration, put all of the group member's names into a container and draw out one each. Then write a note of

appreciation to share with that member of your group. Some people may wish to write them on cards they make or special paper they find. It's a beautiful gift to receive and have forever. You will leave with a note of appreciation from a group member written especially for you, capturing the loving essence of who you really are. If you are a small group maybe do one for each member.

Exercise Ideas for Facilitators

Week Two

Trust Exercise: Have everyone in the group walk and mingle. Stop in front of each individual and look into that person's eyes for at least thirty to forty-five seconds. While doing so, both ask yourselves, "Do I trust this person?" This is best done in silence. After everyone has had a chance to do it with each member of the group, sit and write how the exercise felt for you. Then have a circle where individually people tell how he or she experienced the exercise and what they learned about themselves from it. Everyone has the choice of "passing" if they so wish. However, remember that the more you show of yourself, the better you and others will understand you. There is a related practice you may want to take home with you called Beginning Anew. Beginning Anew is an opportunity to practice loving speech and deep listening with those we love. It has saved many families. To learn about this practice, see Appendix F.

Week Three

"Tell me about yourself" Exercise: Have people split into pairs and sit facing each other in a private space. One person asks the other, "Tell me about yourself" and then listens with no interruptions. When the person stops speaking, wait at least thirty seconds before asking, "Tell me *more* about yourself," and continue to do this until ten minutes have passed. Then the other person has their turn. This can be a very hard exercise for many people, as it could be the first time in their life that they have really been totally listened to. It is also hard because it may be the first time in their life that they have listened without making any comments. Then have a circle where individually people tell how he or she experienced the exercise and what they learned about themselves from it. Everyone has the choice of "passing" if they so wish. However, remember that the more you show of yourself the better you and others will understand you.

Week Four

Action Exercise: Divide a page into two columns. On the left hand–side get everyone to write out a list of ten things they would like to change in their lives. Then ask them to write out a list of ten things they would like to do for other people. On the right–hand side ask them to write out the first step (action) towards doing these things. It could be as simple as a phone call.

Week Five

"What am I tolerating in my life?" Exercise: Get everyone to write a list out of what they are tolerating in their lives in this moment. It could be a person, a job, a relationship, something in their home or something as simple as a broken nail! Then get them to write out, beside each of their tolerations, what their next step

would be to making a change. Have everyone sit in a circle afterwards and, as they wish, share some of their tolerations and next
actions.

Week Six

"What were some of your victories last week?" Exercise: Get
everyone to share individually at least one mindful victory (a success) they had during the past week.

Week Seven

The Mother/Father Exercise: Ask everyone to think of one person they have issues with—it could be their mother or father or
sibling or partner or someone they work with or whomever. Ask
them to write at the top "Fifty things I like about ... (filling in the
name of the person)". Ask them to first write down ten things they
like about that person. Then ask them to write out ten more things.
This is a difficult exercise for many people. Ask them to take the
exercise home and during the week to write out thirty more things.
Ask everyone to share afterwards how the exercise was for them
and how they felt. Make sure everyone brings back the list with
them the next week.

Week Eight

Hugging Meditation Exercise: Have everyone cross out the
name at the top of their list (from the previous week's exercise) and
then read out the list to everyone. Suggest everyone take their list
home and put it in a prominent place to see daily. Then have

everyone practice Hugging Meditation. Stand in two lines facing each other and have an extra person at the end (this is the observer). Have everyone exchange a Mindful Hug—embracing the other person in two arms, while breathing in and out slowly three times. As you breathe in, say to yourself, "You are in my arms," and as you breathe out, say to yourself, "And I am so happy." After each hug have everyone move one place to the right, always leaving one person at the end. This allows everyone to receive a hug from everyone else.

Mindful Way Center Information Sheet

We are a diverse secular group of people who practice mindfulness. Our practice encourages the importance and the joy of bringing mindful awareness into all aspects of our lives. We practice mindful living.

We have a thirty-minute semi-guided sitting meditation followed by ten minutes of walking meditation, then mindful tea, a mindfulness teaching, and discussion. Meditation has immeasurable benefits. It helps overcome stress and anxiety, improves relationships, solves problems and reduces ill health. Through meditation we discover the powerful potential we all have in our mind to overcome our suffering and find joy and peace. Everyone can learn to meditate. If you can relax, you can meditate. When you relax completely there is total silence. This overwhelming sense of tranquility is really all meditation is about. Simply sit or kneel on a cushion/ chair, watch your breath, empty yourself, and you will experience silence and a deep satisfying sense of peace.

Sitting meditation is not to achieve, but to be yourself and to smile. If your sitting position seems uncomfortable, don't be afraid

What characterizes a Community of Mindful Living (or a Mindfulness Practice Community), is the practice of the Five Mindfulness Practice Trainings. We cannot call our community a Mindfulness Practice Center when we do not live according to the Five Mindfulness Trainings.

–THICH NHAT HANH

175

MINDFUL WAY CENTER
INFORMATION SHEET

Walking on water
is considered a
miracle. I think
the real miracle is
to walk on Earth.

–THICH NHAT HANH

Whether you are
in Hell or in
Heaven depends
entirely on the
way you walk.

–THICH NHAT HANH

Kiss the earth
with your feet.
Bring the Earth
your love and
happiness.

–THICH NHAT HANH

to change your position mindfully and quietly while you are in meditation. Breathe consciously, this is to know that the air is entering your body (watch the rising of the stomach—like a newborn baby) and to breathe out consciously is to know that your body is exchanging air (watch the falling of your stomach—like a balloon deflating). Follow the guided meditation and combine the words "In" and "Out" with your in- and out-breath.

When doing walking meditation, we walk very slowly together in a circle, keeping pace with others. When you breathe in, place one foot on the ground. When you breathe out, place the other foot on the ground. Your breathing should be natural. Match your steps to your breath, not the other way around. We can use the words "In" and "Out" or this verse: "I have arrived" (In-breath/one foot), "I am home" (Out-breath/other foot), "in the Here" (In-breath/one foot) and "in the Now" (Out-breath/other foot).

We meet once a week on ___ evenings (afternoons/mornings) and begin promptly at ___ p.m./a.m. Please arrive at least ten minutes early. If you do arrive late, please join us very mindfully and quietly, so as not to disturb others who are meditating. The first time we meet in a new month we recite the Five Mindfulness Practice Trainings together. Our group is self-supporting. We suggest a heartfelt contribution. We invite you, if you wish, to be our guest on your first visit.

Walking Meditation

In walking meditation, we coordinate our steps with our breath. We breathe naturally and take one, two, or three steps for each in–breath and one, two, or three steps for each out–breath. When doing walking meditation indoors, for example as a part of our session of sitting meditation, we take one step with each in–breath and one step with each out–breath.

When we walk outdoors, we may want to walk more naturally so that we take perhaps two, three, or even four steps with each in–breath or out–breath. While walking, practice conscious breathing by noticing your breath and the number of steps you take as you breathe in and out. We can practice walking meditation by counting steps or by using words. If you take three steps for an in–breath, you may want to say silently, "In, in, in." If you also take three steps for your out–breath, you can say, "Out, out, out," or for four steps, "Out, out, out, out."

Don't try to control your breathing. Allow your lungs as much time and air as they need. Simply be mindful of both your breath and your steps. When you walk uphill or downhill, the number of steps per breath will change. Always follow the needs of your lungs. Don't try to control your breathing or your walking.

Just observe them. You can also do jogging meditation this way.

You can also practice walking meditation using the lines of a poem. In Zen Buddhism, poetry and practice always go together.

> I have arrived.
> I am home
> in the here,
> In the now.
> I am solid.
> I am free.
> In the ultimate
> I dwell.

Or you can take words from the poem: "Arrived, arrived, arrived. Home, home, home," or "Solid, solid. Free, free," or "Here. Now."

You can practice walking meditation when going from one meeting or one building to another, between the parking lot and your office, or up and down the stairs. When you walk anywhere, allow yourself enough time to practice.

Taking steps on our beautiful planet can bring much happiness. Be aware of your foot, the ground, and the connection between them. Walking mindfully on the Earth can restore our peace and harmony, and it can restore the Earth's peace and harmony as well. If your steps are peaceful, the world will have peace. If you can make one peaceful step, then peace is possible.

Peace Treaty and Note*

Peace Treaty

In Order That We May Live Long and Happily Together, In Order That We May Continually Develop and Deepen Our Love and Understanding, We the Undersigned, Vow to Observe and Practice the Following:

I, the one who is angry, agree to:

1. Refrain from saying or doing anything that might cause further damage or escalate the anger.
2. Not suppress my anger.
3. Practice breathing and taking refuge in the island of myself.
4. Calmly, within twenty-four hours, tell the one who has made me angry about my anger and suffering, either verbally or by delivering a Peace Note.
5. Ask for an appointment for later in the week (e.g. Friday evening) to discuss this matter more thoroughly either verbally or by Peace Note.
6. Not say: "I am not angry. It's okay. I am not suffering. There is

* see Thich Nhat Hanh, *Touching Peace* (Berkeley, CA: Parallax Press, 1992).

nothing to be angry about, at least not enough to make me angry."

7. Practice breathing and looking deeply into my daily life—while sitting, lying down, standing, and walking—in order to see:

   a. the ways I myself have been unskillful at times.

   b. how I have hurt the other person because of my own habit energy.

   c. how the strong seed of anger in me is the primary cause of my anger.

   d. how the other person's suffering, which waters the seed of my anger, is the secondary cause.

   e. how the other person is only seeking relief from his or her own suffering.

   f. that as long as the other person suffers, I cannot be truly happy.

8. Apologize immediately, without waiting until Friday evening, as soon as I realize my unskillfulness and lack of mindfulness.

9. Postpone the Friday meeting if I do not feel calm enough to meet with the other person.

I, the one who has made the other angry, agree to:

1. Respect the other person's feelings, not ridicule him or her, and allow enough time for him or her to calm down.

2. Not press for an immediate discussion.

3. Confirm the other person's request for a meeting, either verbally or by note, and assure him or her that I will be there.

4. Practice breathing and taking refuge in the island of myself to see how:

   a. I have seeds of unkindness and anger as well as the habit energy to make the other person unhappy.

b. I have mistakenly thought that making the other person suf–
fer would relieve my own suffering.

c. by making him or her suffer, I make myself suffer.

5. Apologize as soon as I realize my unskillfulness and lack of
mindfulness, without making any attempt to justify myself
and without waiting until the Friday meeting.

We Vow, with Lord Buddha as Witness and the Mindful Presence
of the Sangha, to Abide by These Articles and to Practice Whole-
heartedly. We Invoke the Three Gems for Protection and to Grant
Us Clarity and Confidence.

Signed,_____

the_____ Day of_____

in the Year_____ in _____ .

★ ★

Peace Note

Date:_____

Time:_____

Dear_____ ,

This morning (afternoon), you said (did) something that made me
very angry. I suffered very much. I want you to know this. You said
(did):

Please let us both look at what you said (did) and examine the
matter together in a calm and open manner this Friday evening.

Yours, not very happy right now,

_____

*Beginning Anew**

Beginning Anew creates harmony and keeps communication open. Those who live together can practice it once a week. Some families like to practice on Friday evening, so they are renewed to enjoy their weekend even more.

We come together and sit in a circle, in the center of which is a small pot of flowers or a single flower. Someone is the bell master. We begin with a few minutes of silence. Then a person who wishes to speak gets up, walks mindfully to the center, picks up the vase of flowers and takes it back to her seat and places it before them. The flowers are a reminder of our freshness and our desire to speak in a loving way from our heart. As long as that person has the flower, only she has the right to speak. While she is speaking, everyone follows their breathing and listens. When she has finished, she replaces the flower in the center and another person can go to the center, bring the flower back to their seat and speak. While she speaks, everyone in the circle follows their breathing and listens. The bell master may want to invite the bell to sound between each speaker or after several people have spoken.

There are four areas of Beginning Anew. We don't need to prac-

* see Thich Nhat Hanh, *Teachings on Love* (Berkeley, CA: Parallax Press, 1998).

tice all four, but it's always good to start with flower watering. This is the first part of Beginning Anew, expressing appreciation. We acknowledge the other person, perhaps something they have done in the past week that we noticed and appreciated. We nourish the flower in them and allow it to bloom. The second part of Beginning Anew is an opportunity to express regret for something we have done, perhaps something we did that might have been hurtful, thoughtless, or unkind, or something which might have led to mis-understanding. The third part of the practice is to express hurt. This can sometimes be difficult. Sometimes people prefer to do it alone, just with the other person and perhaps a third person as facilitator, rather than to do it with the whole group. We use mindful speech, and are careful not to be accusing. The other person cannot respond at that time, but can have a chance later on, at an agreed upon time, perhaps in a few days or in a week at the next session of Beginning Anew. This gives each person a chance to reflect on how they may have contributed to the situation before they meet again to speak. The fourth part of Beginning Anew is to express something we want to say that is in our heart, something that has made us sad, that may be affecting our behavior, or something that has brought us joy. The practice of Beginning Anew brings us lightness, energy, and joy, and a greater capacity to transform what is negative in us, as well as to transform the situation outside.

Acknowledgments

Igive a deep bow of gratitude to the Most Venerable Thich Nhat Hanh (Thay) for his Mindfulness Trainings and to the late Jim Quinn for his simple LifeStream teachings. It is with great gratitude that I have found much insightful knowledge from these teachers and all living beings.

Thich Nhat Hanh is the one who has taught me mindfulness. His generosity and wisdom inspire me daily. Jim Quinn taught me the "key" and also the "two secrets." For him, the "key" to a happy life was to center every day. What Jim called centering is what I call Mindful Meditation. So the "key" in *A Mindful Way* is daily Mindful Meditation—a time to allow the mind to stop and just be.

Jim's "two secrets" were to each day say to yourself, " I love myself, I accept myself, even though I sometimes do not understand myself" and then, "I love you, I accept you, even though I sometimes do not understand you." After all, happiness is a function of acceptance. What Jim called the "two secrets," I call Mindful Memoirs (understanding and accepting yourself) and Mindful Gratitudes (understanding and accepting others and the world around you).

Another great source of inspiration for this book has been Julia Cameron's *The Artist's Way*. Spiritual paths come from different directions but they all lead to the same destination.

I wish to express my deepest gratitude to my dear husband John for his constant loving support throughout our life together. I also thank him for rereading this book a number of times and encouraging me often during the time I was writing it. My thanks also go to Mark, my second son, for his skillful editing of *A Mindful Way*. I am also thankful to my other children David, Timothy, Larissa, Angela, and Amanda for their continued love, encouragement, and support in so many ways.

It has been my honor and pleasure to be with each and every one of you on your individual or collective journey into the realm of present moment awareness.

In gratitude,

Jeanie

Parallax Press, a nonprofit organization, publishes books on engaged Buddhism and the practice of mindfulness by Thich Nhat Hanh and other authors. All of Thich Nhat Hanh's work is available at our online store and in our free catalog. For a copy of the catalog, please contact:

Parallax Press
www.parallax.org
P.O. Box 7355, Berkeley, CA 94707
Tel: 510 525-0101

Individuals and families are invited to practice the art of mindful living in the tradition of Thich Nhat Hanh at retreat communities in France and the United States. For information, please visit www.plumvillage.org or contact:

Plum Village
13 Martineau
33580 Dieulivol, France
info@plumvillage.org

Green Mountain Dharma Center
P.O. Box 182
Hartland Four Corners, VT 05049
mfmaster@vermontel.net
Tel: 802 436-1103

Deer Park Monastery
2499 Melru Lane
Escondido, CA 92026
deerpark@plumvillage.org
Tel: 760 291-1003

For a worldwide directory of Sanghas practicing in the tradition of Thich Nhat Hanh, please visit www.iamhome.org.